HANDLEY PAGE

FORTY YEARS ON, 1909-1949

UPON THE ASSETS SIDE, FREEHOLD LAND, BUILDINGS, ETC.

Handley Page, the first limited liability company to be constituted exclusively for the design and manufacture of aeroplanes, had its original works at Barking, near London.

HANDLEY PAGE

FORTY YEARS ON, 1909-1949

At Um el Surab, the Handley stood majestic on the grass,
with Bristols and 9A, like fledglings beneath its spread of wings.

Round it admired the Arabs, saying:
"Indeed, and at last, they have sent us THE aeroplane,
of which these things were foals."

Before night, rumours of Feisal's resource went over
Jebel Druse and the hollow of Hauran, telling people
that the balance was weighed on our side.

Lawrence of Arabia in *Seven Pillars of Wisdom*.

FONTHILL

Fonthill Media Limited
www.fonthillmedia.com
office@fonthillmedia.com

This edition first published in the United Kingdom 2012

British Library Cataloguing in Publication Data
A catalogue record for this book is available from the British Library

ISBN 978-1-78155-007-6 (PRINT)
ISBN 978-1-78155-148-6 (E-BOOK)

Printed and bound in England

Connect with us
f facebook.com/fonthillmedia t twitter.com/fonthillmedia

Introduction

to this 2012 edition

When this book was originally published in 1949, to record and celebrate the first forty years of the Handley Page story, the British aircraft industry of which the company was a leading member was younger, much larger and far more diverse than the one which survives today. It was possible at that time to identify as many as twenty-seven different, mostly independent firms, the most important of which had been born in the early pioneering years prior to the First World War, while the men who had begun it all, household names such as Thomas Sopwith, Richard Fairey, Geoffrey de Havilland and the redoubtable Frederick Handley Page, were still very much in control.

Now, four decades and two wars later, that industry was a major component of Britain's manufacturing sector, with a workforce running into hundreds of thousands and drawing offices which were continually creating new designs. Although the great wartime surge that saw vast numbers of aircraft flowing off the production lines was now at an end, the exigencies engendered by the Korean War and, more lastingly, the Cold War had continued to bring substantial orders to the leading companies. However, with technology continuing to advance, making aeroplanes ever more complex — and hence more expensive, yet with the nation wishing to retain its position as a leading air power, increasingly heavy burdens were being placed on defence budgets. The problem was not diminished by the well-established system which, in response to each new MOD requirement, might see several competing companies designing, manufacturing and test-flying their own prototype, each project being supported by the grant of a government contract. This was all very well in pre-war days, when aeroplanes were relatively simple and relatively cheap, but by the fifties it had become a wasteful multiplication of resources which could no longer be afforded. While, on the ministerial side, there was a need for military procurement to be more rigorously controlled, by 1957 the government of the day had also concluded that strong action was required to replace the many-headed monster of an industry by one which ideally would consist of no more than two large concerns. Since the existing companies showed no signs of willingness to abandon their cherished independence, force would clearly have to be applied. The weapon which the government proposed to use was its power to grant or to withhold new military contracts, which in any case were now rather scarcer than in the past. The message soon became clear: merge or no more orders.

The history of the relationship between government and the aircraft industry has not always been a happy one. With a great part of the latter's income deriving from public money, there can be no disputing government's right — indeed duty — to exert some control over the public money spent in that quarter, but the industry had reason to fear for the consequences of this official 'interference' in their lawful pursuance of trade. The infamous Defence White Paper issued that same year of 1957 by the responsible Minister, Duncan Sandys, with its declaration that henceforth there would be 'no more manned combat aircraft', represents perhaps the direst example both of politicians' limited grasp of aeronautical realities and of the malign effects their policies have had on this country's aircraft industry over the years, while the cancellation by the Wilson government in 1965 of Hawker-Siddeley's P1154 (the 'supersonic Harrier'), its HS681 VSTOL military transport and BAC's TSR2 must run it a close second. (There would have been a fourth — Concorde — had the French not refused to allow this joint project to be abandoned).

Nevertheless, with the government in a strong position, the companies reluctantly conceded and embarked on a series of complex negotiations. In the greatest upheaval the industry had ever experienced, these culminated in 1960 in what were grimly referred to in aviation circles at the time as 'shotgun weddings': two airframe manufacturers only, in the form of the British Aircraft Corporation and — already existing, but in a too loosely-bound form — the Hawker-Siddeley Group. The government had got what it wanted.

Well, almost: the nuptials ended with some untidy leftovers. Westland was omitted, to become the sole helicopter manufacturer, a job which both of the two big consortiums had shunned; Shorts, in Northern Ireland and more-or-less nationalised anyway, was left alone. And there was Handley Page.

The latter had not stood aloof from the merger talks. It had three cards in its hand. The strongest was provided by the Victor, which had now joined the Vulcan and Valiant in equipping the nation's nuclear deterrent force. The twin-engined Herald short-range airliner looked good and at that time was the RAF's preferred choice for its new communications aircraft. Thirdly, another airliner, the Jetstream, was showing considerable promise.

These proved not to be enough. When it came down to it, the negotiations foundered on Sir Frederick's refusal to accept the Hawker Siddeley valuation of Handley Page shares and negotiations came to naught. When, pursuing its uncompromising policy, the Government then cancelled a contract for more Victors and failed to award one at all for Heralds, the die was cast and Handley Page was left to plough a lonely furrow in a hostile world.

Sir Frederick died in 1962, while the company which he had formed struggled on for another seven years until, in the sixtieth year of its foundation it succumbed to the inevitable and went into voluntary liquidation. A number of Heralds had been sold and the Jetstream proved a success, though later on and in other hands, but it was the Victor which undoubtedly represented HP's greatest post-war achievement. Although overshadowed by the Vulcan, it formed a significant part of this country's V-Bomber Force during the long stand-off with the Eastern Bloc which we know as the Cold War.

Finally, at the very end of their service lives, the two types jointly enjoyed their finest hour when in 1982 eleven Victor tankers formed the vital refuelling squadron which, in the memorable and extended logistical exercise above the waters of the South Atlantic, sent one lone Vulcan on its 8000-mile round trip to the Falklands and back, to perform its successful mission of bombing the Port Stanley runway and denying its use to the Argentinians' fast jets.

Malcolm Hall

Publisher's Note

This text, captions and images was originally produced in 1949 as a Handley Page marketing brochure celebrating 40 years from the Company's formation. It was printed on War Economy paper, and the quality of reproduction was not high. The illustrations in this book have been reproduced from the original brochure to the best possible quality. Unfortunately photographic prints of the original photographs were not available.

The cheery Pathé News-type commentary is typical of the time, and the original text has been left exactly as it was. It seems that the author, presumably a marketing person at Handley Page, was of an older generation, for he refers to the Second World War as the 'World War', and the First World War as the 'Great War'. The reader should bear in mind that this optimistic and chirpy piece of promotion is aviation history preserved in aspic.

Foreword

by

Sir Frederick Handley Page, CBE, Hon. FRAeS
Chairman and Managing Director, Handley Page Ltd.

Here in the twentieth century, in the midst of this changing scene of scientific achievement and mechanical progress it is difficult for us to gauge the place which our era will ultimately hold in the history of mankind. It may well be as great a time in material achievement as that of the Greeks in speculative thought twenty-five centuries ago.

In no sphere of human activity has development been so rapid as in the art of flying. Less than fifty years ago, the Wright brothers made the first power-driven, controlled. mechanical flight. Today, not only has, a new science been evolved, but also its principles have been developed and applied so that a third dimension of travel has been made available to the world at large and still offers new vistas of great future developments.

Through the past four decades of practical flying, run many stories of pioneer work done, of disappointments and successes, but, with it all, continuing progress. Here in this book, is one story of the many which form the great picture as a whole.

To those who have taken part, it will be interesting as a reminder of what already has been done in the past. For those still engaged in this field and, for those who are just entering it, there lies before them an immense vista of scientific discovery and engineering application as great, if not greater, than of at any time in the history of this new art. To all those this book is commended as a brief account and in the hope that it may be an inspiration.

Pigs Might Fly

by
Lord Brabazon of Tara PC, MC, FRAeS

Forty years is a long time. It is the whole of aviation, from its birth to its present position. H.P., as an individual, would have been a tremendous figure in whatever walk of life he chose; for he is big in every way — in stature, in imagination, in pertinacity and in character generally.

Lucky are we all that he chose the province of aviation and has been our friend and help over many years, and lucky indeed the nation that, in its direst troubles, it had his great firm already existing to pull us out of trouble.

It is indeed a man's job to run a big factory under any condition, but with the Government poking its finger into every part of a business from design to operation, it must drive ordinary people nearly insane. H.P., however, has a natural good humour that overrides everything and yet still turns to give attention outside to all those bodies concerned with aviation, such as the Royal Aeronautical Society and the Royal Aero Club, which he has helped so much and which owe him such a great debt of gratitude.

I go back myself to those early days when H.P. made a monoplane with swept-back wings. Did he dream then with prescience of "mach" numbers? There was no help or hindrance then from Governments — nor help from anyone else. All who tried to solve the problems of flight were just amiable lunatics. We have not changed; we are still amiable, I hope.

My first flights were launched ones from a rail. A weight which descended from a pylon helped us off by a complicated system of pulleys; if we ever got up we landed on skids. It all sounds very absurd but, just as the swept-back wing has come back, so, I believe, launching and landing on skids will come back again. Think of the saving in "useful weight". I never liked the rail, because it always took a long time to set up into the eye of the wind. Any wind over five mph and back we went to the shed! But when we had got it perfect, the wind changed and we had to start again: most exasperating!

The picture of me in the first Short machine shows a very historic incident in flight. The *Daily Mirror*, with much imagination, came down and asked me to take a pig up to break the old adage "pigs might fly". This noble animal — you can tell it, it being the one in the basket — should have been pampered in life and preserved in death in the British Museum. But all that happened was that it was sold next day slightly above its market price. Why, I never understood; I could not have improved its taste by taking it on its historic flight.

Those were great days: days of trial and error, of hopes, excitement and laughter. Do not ever think we were heroic for we very seldom left the ground; our flights were mostly of imagination.

How near we were I well remember with a particular Voisin I had. I knew that if I could not persuade its engine to turn at 1130 instead of 1100 rpm it would never think of getting up. But, if it was feeling good, then it was all right for a hop, though only with my coat off, no boots and half a gallon of petrol. A poor "useful load"!

Flight was not born in the laboratory, nor for gain. It was born by the persistence, imagination and enterprise of individuals whom nothing could stop. That those early workshops, where these contraptions were put together. eventually became almost armament factories, just happened. It was never planned. But it was lucky for the country that it turned out that way.

Handley Page Ltd — a great firm, known and honoured throughout the world, with a great and worthy chief. So may they both long continue. They are both national institutions.

Almost Prehistoric

The story of Handley Page Limited, the first Company to be constituted exclusively for the design and manufacture of aeroplanes, is a cross-section of aviation since it emerged, early in the twentieth century, from the speculative to the scientific, experimental and operational stages.

Handley Page history started within a short time of man's conquest of the air: it began in the pioneer days when only an enlightened few believed in the immense potentialities of heavier-than-air flight.

During the intervening four decades, the Company has been in the forefront of aeronautical progress and endeavour.

It has achieved much in the realms of aviation. A great reputation has been created by high-performance Handley Page aeroplanes, both military and civil. Throughout the world they are renowned for safety, strength and size.

By research, trial, tribulation, faith and courage, the Handley Page Company proved that the big, multi-engined aeroplane was feasible and confounded the many sceptics who contended that it was not: it persisted in progressive design which achieved always a high degree of inherent stability in its aircraft; its famous slotted-wing has had world-wide adoption and is the biggest single contribution to air-safety since man first flew; it pioneered Britain's overseas airlines thirty years ago: its production methods, emulated wherever aircraft are built, are the criteria of efficiency. As early as 1906, at the age of 21, Frederick Handley Page was one of a small band of pioneers interested in flying.

He founded and is still the directing power of Handley Page Ltd., the great organisation which he has commanded throughout its forty successful years. By profession an electrical engineer, he joined the Royal Aeronautical Society in 1908 and was one of the members who re-organised it in 1910 when the Society became a fully constituted scientific organisation with Fellows and Associates in the recognised form.

By trial and error methods, these pioneers were preparing the way for the great strides which aviation has made during the twentieth century. For, less than fifty years ago, even the fundamental principles of flight were speculative.

GREAT EXPECTATIONS
Handley Page's stand at the London Aero Show in 1909.

The Handley Page organisation was founded in 1908 and it was incorporated as a limited liability company on the 17th of June, 1909, when the first British works to be constructed exclusively for the manufacture of aircraft was erected at Barking, near London.

It is difficult to realise to-day the utter lack of all aviation facilities forty odd years ago. There were no experimental data on which to base calculations pertaining to the strength or flying capacity of aeroplanes. Theoretical calculations were imperfectly understood. From a little empirical knowledge, it was not possible to work except by rule of number methods.

Aeroplanes, when completed, lacked sufficient power: engines were heavy for their horsepower output. It was difficult to fly the finished product; few trained pilots existed; the art of flying was practically unknown; there were no real aerodromes from which to fly. And so, one had a would-be airman not knowing how to fly, trying to get airborne from an inadequate field in a machine whose capabilities and strength were unknown factors and whose engine might cease to function at any moment.

BARKING WORKS, 1909
"Your Company is keeping well to the fore in the development of new types."

It is small wonder that the Company's progress in these conditions was slow. Most of the early experimental work was conducted with gliders not only because of the imperfection of the early internal combustion engine, but also in view of the heavy odds against long immunity from disaster. For take-off, a steep hillock which covered an old rubbish dump on the Barking marshes was convenient.

Some powered aeroplanes were constructed in the Barking works. They had swept-back wings as do the supersonic aircraft of today. A monoplane, whose wing shape and colour caused it to be known as Blue Bird, was built in 1909 and was followed by a biplane.

A separate section of the works was devoted to research into the design and manufacture of propellers at the end of that year. The Willows airship which flew from London to Cardiff in 1910 was fitted with a Handley Page propeller.

Although 1910 opened with calamity for the new company — part of the works being destroyed during a gale and two experimental aircraft in course of construction for clients having to be rebuilt — ill-fortune did not discourage progress. A monoplane with a horizontally-opposed twin-cylinder engine was built for demonstration flights and exhibition at the Olympia aircraft show, together with a selection of Handley Page propellers.

Another monoplane which was exhibited by the Company at Olympia in the following year was less efficient than handsome. Its abandonment for a new design resulted in Handley Page's first big success. This, because of the non-rusting composition with which its surface was treated, was known both as the Yellow Peril and Antiseptic. Its swept-back wings had a span of 35 feet, it had a 50 hp Gnome engine enclosed in a cowl. and it was capable of 60 mph. Like many of its contemporaries the Yellow Peril crashed. On being reconstructed and improved in 1912 it flew across London, following the course of the Thames, to Brooklands.

Several other aircraft were built and flown during the three years before the outbreak of war in 1914. All achieved a high degree of inherent stability, the quality which always has been the fundamental basis of Handley Page aircraft design.

But it was a crash which eliminated a more powerful Handley Page monoplane, fitted with a 80 hp Gnome engine, from the military trials of 1912. Another disaster, which killed both the Naval pilot and the founder's chief assistant at the time, prevented the British Admiralty from adopting an aeroplane of the same class.

NO ATOMIC WORRIES.
Even when completed, aeroplanes of 1910 lacked sufficient driving-force, engines being heavy for their power output.

THE PILOT HAD WIDE VISION
Blue Bird of 1909 had swept-back wings, as do the modern supersonics.

PROPELLER DIVISION
Although up the Barking Creek, these were not rubber paddles.

It was in this year that the Company moved to larger works at Cricklewood, in north-west London, and at first occupied a factory area of 20,000 sq. feet, roughly double that at Barking. At this time, the British Government was stimulated to greater enterprise and interest in the development of flying by the importance which was given to their military air arms by Continental powers and by persistent Press and Parliamentary campaigns in Britain. Handley Page Ltd., had specialised in the production of Service aircraft since its removal to Cricklewood. With war-clouds gathering, it contracted to supply five biplanes to the War Office.

Independent experiments continued and a biplane of remarkable stability was produced in 1913. It had a 100 hp Anzani engine and was capable of 73 mph. Acquired by the late Mr. Rowland Ding, it took part in various aviation meetings and in it he flew Princess Lowenstein Wertheim across the Channel. When war began in 1914, this aircraft was bought by the Royal Naval Air Service and stationed for training and defence purposes at Hendon. Its offensive and defensive potentialities were limited to one Webley revolver, worn by the pilot. Its swept-back wings, although contributing to stability, nearly caused its destruction. During a patrol, the biplane was mistaken by London's defenders for a Taube and riddled with bullets, but without serious effect. After an accident on the ground at Chingford RNAS Station in August 1915, this aircraft was written-off, or, in the official phraseology of those days, "deleted".

SWEPT-BACK IN THE EDWARDIAN MODE
Handley Page's monoplane at London's Olympia in 1911 had interesting aerodynamic features and fine craftsmanship. Persistent engine trouble made it an unsuccessful flier.

AN EARLY SUCCESS
Over London from Barking to Brooklands flew the triumphant Yellow Peril. This inherently stable monoplane was piloted by Edward Petre — Peter-the-Painter, to his friends.

MONOPLANE VINTAGE 1910
Horizontal twin-cylinders powered its demonstration flights and intrigued aviation enthusiasts at that year's British Aero Show.

LAST LAP AT A MILE-A-MINUTE
Because of its virulent colour, the 1911 Yellow Peril was known also as the
Antiseptic. It had fifty horse-power and a 35-feet swept-back wing-span.

A steady progression in the size, power and speed of Handley Page aircraft
reached pre-war culmination in a biplane which was begun in 1914 for competition in
a proposed Trans-Atlantic flight. Although diverted by hostilities from its destined
mission, this aircraft, equipped with a 200 hp Salmson engine, was completed after
the Great War started.

MILITARY TRIALS

In 1912, this monoplane was built for the military trials
which were held on Salisbury Plain. Pilot and passenger
sat side-by-side.

CROSS-CHANNEL BIPLANE

This very stable 1913 biplane flew with its vertical tail-fin
removed. Mr Rowland Ding took Princess Lowenstein
Wertheim (pictured) across the English Channel in it.

The World's First Big Aeroplane

In modern warfare, the employment of aircraft as independent striking forces is well established. Today it may be forgotten that, at the beginning of the Great War, military opinion was almost unanimous in the belief that the aeroplane's sole spheres of usefulness were in reconnaissance and as artillery auxiliaries. A general view was that if air attack on ground objectives became a factor worthy of serious study, its agent must be the airship and not the heavier-than-air machine. This attitude is understandable when it is remembered that in 1914 no efficient bomb-release mechanism was in use; the margin of lift available for projectiles was so small that an aircraft's armament was limited to a few hand grenades carried in the aviator's pockets, a light bomb or two slung about his person and possibly a rifle or revolver. Even though the Royal Naval Air Service aeroplanes were more highly-powered than the aircraft of the British military wing, difficulty was experienced when taking off fully-loaded with, comparatively speaking, the bare necessities.

Thus the scepticism of military and naval authorities was well-founded in respect of the offensive powers of aircraft.

It was entirely due to the vigour and persistence with which the aircraft constructors increased the reliability and load-carrying capabilities of their aeroplanes that a change in the official attitude occurred.

No name is better known than that of Handley Page in regard to this progressive development. Its bombers justly may be claimed to have made possible the creation of an independent strategy of air warfare.

Natural it was that the Admiralty, charged with coastal defence, took most interest in the new offensive arm's development possibilities. On its approach to Handley Page at the end of 1914 with regard to the construction of four, large, twin-engined biplanes, able to transport an effective load of projectiles, the Company devoted an exhaustive year to the task.

No big aircraft of the specified type existed at the time; this was the beginning of the multi-engined design.

"BLOODY PARALYSER"
The multi-engined bomber — a Handley Page — made its debut in 1915.

Rear-Admiral Sir Murray Sueter (Commodore, as he was then, and Director of the Air Department of the Admiralty) had placed the order for these aircraft which were to be fitted with two Sunbeam 150 hp engines and able to carry six 112 lb bombs, a crew of two and to have a top speed of 72 mph. Plans for building large aircraft already had been turned down by the War Office and Sueter's immediate reward was to be called "the biggest damned fool in the Navy".

Events silenced the critics. The resultant Handley Page aeroplanes satisfied the Navy's demand for a "bloody paralyser".

Thus, military requirements dictated the type of aircraft which made the Handley Page name universally famous. To this day, many people throughout the world call any large aircraft "a Handley Page". It is the big aircraft, of whatever make, which is synonymous with the Handley Page name the world over.

On the 18th December, 1915, the twin-engined O/100, forerunner of the famous O/400, flew for the first time. And, as the first successful big bomber ever to be produced, it was the true sire of the world's modern brood of heavy bombers and giant military and civil transports. It proved to all beholders that big aircraft were not an impossibility.

Intervening months had been spent in experiment and research, testing and trial, revision and improvement. No holiday was taken by the enthusiastic Handley Page organisation — even on Sundays.

Exhaustive mechanical and structural tests had been conducted both on the materials to be used and on the completed parts. Everything had been carefully

SIRE OF THE MODERN BROOD
Aerial giants of the Great War, the Handley Page O/400's were the world's first
heavy bombers.

lightened to save any unnecessary ounce of weight. Simultaneously, a long series of
research experiments had been conducted in a "wind tunnel" on models of the planes
and bodies which were to be used. Everything had been most carefully tested and tried.

Production of the world's first big aeroplane and its first real bomber had been well
worth such unremittant effort and adequate reward.

Rolls Royce Eagle engines had been installed with substantial benefit to
performance. Other alterations, additions and experiments also were necessary
subsequently; this was to be expected with an aircraft whose like in size and
performance had neither been known or flown before. Substantially, though, it was
the same aircraft which finished the war as Britain's standard heavy bomber.

In operational service, it had extraordinary stability, was easily controlled and able
to maintain flight with one engine out of action. As was natural, the revolutionary
O/100 became pre-eminent in the bombing sphere. Forty were built. They dispensed
with the heavy armour-plate which had protected the petrol tank and parts of the
fuselage of the first bomber. Squadrons operated from the Naval Air Service base
at Dunkirk. With more than a ton of bombs and a maximum speed of 97 mph, they
attacked targets inside Germany and systematically bombed Ostend, Zeebrugge,
Bruges and other haunts of the U-boat along the Belgian coast.

A direct development of the O/100 bomber was the O/400 which followed upon
the introduction of certain modifications; its Rolls Royce engines had been improved,
armour-plating removed and petrol tanks placed in the fuselage instead of behind
the engines.

Formation of the Independent Air Force in 1918 under the command of Lord
Trenchard (a Major-General at that time) was a logical development which was
coincidental with this proof of the aeroplane as an offensive war weapon. Its heavy-
bomber squadrons being composed of O/400s, this force was responsible for the
intense bombing of the German Rhineland towns. Some six hundred of these big
Handley Page aircraft were ordered and approximately four hundred built before the

"BIGGEST DAMNED FOOL IN THE NAVY" This was the reputation which Rear-Admiral Sir Murray Sueter (middle) gained when in 1914, he ordered the first big bomber for the RNAS. Subsequently, the HP O/100's triumph silenced his critics. He is seen inspecting Handley Page aircraft construction for the World War. Mr. C. G. Grey, doyen of aeronautical journalists, is on the extreme right.

end of the war. They operated not only against Germany but also attacked the Turks and Bulgarians on the eastern front. Constantinople and enemy troops and shipping being bombed.

An excerpt from a 1918 newspaper indicates the nature of operations which were conducted by these O/400s:

Few know the dangers and difficulties encountered by our bombers on their raids against the U-boat haunts.

The Germans, learning from bitter experience of the damage which the bombers could inflict and the hindrance they caused to the building and repair and coming and going of their submarines, took every possible step to protect their docks, basins and canals, installing powerful searchlights and numerous batteries of anti-aircraft guns, 'flaming onion' rockets and machine guns.

Every attack carried out is pushed through in the face of these defences, the damage going on day and night.

During a recent raid on Zeebrugge our big bombers, with searchlights sweeping the sky and a tornado of 'archie' shells bursting about them, reached their objective and effectively dropped their heavy load of bombs.

One of them was hit by a shell which caught one of the lower planes. The machine was flung headlong by the shock, but the pilot, expecting every moment that the

RUGGED AND STABLE
Hit by a shell and with one wing smashed and the fabric in tatters, a Great War O/400 returned successfully to base from a raid on Zeebrugge. A few nights later, this bomber was attacking the U-boat lairs again.

machine would collapse and drop like a stone, still kept his head, recovered control and flew for home.

The big planes or wings of the machine, built of a frame with fabric drawn tight over and underneath it, stretched away to the right and left and, as they flew, pilot and crew could see that part of this frame was badly smashed and that long ribbons of fabric were streaming and flapping away from it.

It was almost incredible that the machine could carry on. Yet carry on it did, flew home a distance of between 50 and 100 miles (one may not be too exact) and made a good landing.

It was found that the wing had the forward or 'leading edge' and frame smashed as far back as the spars, the rear or 'trailing edge' shot clean away for half its length and the whole of the fabric underneath torn to ribbons.

ROYAL INTEREST
Two future Kings of England saw how Handley Page
pioneered Britain's big bombers during the Great War.

And a few nights afterwards the same machine and the same men were out as good
as ever, 'dropping the eggs' again on the U-boat lairs.

In lighter vein, the O/400 created a world record in 1916 by carrying no less than
twenty passengers and their pilot safely into the air.

Later, the Duke of Windsor, then Prince of Wales, flew over London in an O/400
piloted by Admiral Mark Kerr. In another of these Handley Page bombers, the
present British King (Prince Albert at that time) and his brother, the Prince of Wales,
made their first cross-Channel flight in 1918. It was to Paris and a succession of forced
landings, caused by unfavourable weather conditions, characterised this initiation.

In Russia, Sikorski had developed a big biplane. It was noticeably under-
powered and had a speed of only 65 mph in comparison with the 97 mph of

WOMEN IN INDUSTRY
Queen Alexandra and Princess Victoria, on a visit to the Handley Page works in March 1918, were impressed by the magnificent part which women played in the production of Britain's standard heavy-bombers.

the Handley Page with corresponding horsepower. Before the revolution, the Imperial Russian Government decided to abandon the Sikorski in favour of a Russian-built Handley Page aeroplane. This plan was not brought to fruition, the upheaval in Russia precluding the despatch of necessary data and mechanics from England.

In Italy, a big Caproni aircraft was developed along with a series of other experimental machines. Its evolution came after that of the O/100 but it was the only other successful big Allied aircraft.

It is common knowledge that the German Gotha was modelled on the Handley Page aeroplane which fell into enemy hands intact comparatively early in the war.

This O/100 was one of the first bombers to be delivered from Manston to Dunkirk. Not being sure of his whereabouts en route and seeing French peasants in a field beneath him, the pilot decided that he was over the non-hostile side of the front-line. He landed the big aircraft and with his gunnery officer walked across the field in order to verify his position.

However, a German officer, Major Braune, had hidden his company in a ditch which bordered the field. At the opportune moment, the German troops revealed themselves; a race to the O/100 developed; the rear-portion of the speedier British

BIGGER AND BETTER
Handley Page's V/1500s, in 1918, flew for more than 1,000 miles at 90 mph with a 6½ ton useful load.

aviator was captured as his head and shoulders re-entered the aircraft; an undamaged sample of the world's only successful bomber was in enemy hands.

As the British pilot refused to fly it away, the Germans were forced to dismantle the Handley Page in order to take it to Johanistal, near Berlin. There it was re-erected prior to demonstration before the German Crown Prince. However, it was not only the Allies who made mistakes. Controls were crossed when the O/100 was reconstructed by the enemy. It crashed but not before German technicians had probed some of the secrets of its success.

Super-Handleys

Handley Page's supreme product of the Great War yet was to emerge. With hostilities expected to last a year longer than they did, big bombing attacks were planned against Berlin and other objectives equally far distant from bases in Britain. For them, the four-engined "Super-Handleys" were designed and built.

These mighty warplanes, a type known as V/1500, were bigger than anything which had been seen before; their 126-feet wing span was greater than most aircraft flying today, more than thirty years later.

Each V/1500 had four Rolls Royce engines which, between them, developed a maximum output of 1,400 horsepower. At 90 mph, each big aeroplane was able to carry a crew of six, thirty 250 lb bombs, machine guns and other supplies for a bombing sortie of normal duration. With a smaller load, they could fly non-stop for 1,200 miles.

Such was the remarkable progress made in four years of war that the 13½-ton V/1500 could boast a useful load of 6½ tons, top speed of 100 mph, 1,000-gallon fuel capacity and a 12-hour endurance at between 80-90 gallons per hour.

It was only six months after design work started on the V/1500 that the first flew in April, 1918. A total of 255 of these great aeroplanes was ordered. Three were in readiness for a raid on Berlin when the Armistice came. From all points of view, except the humanitarian, it is unfortunate that the war ended before the Berlin Bomber had an opportunity to justify its creation.

However, it subsequently established a record by carrying forty passengers in flight over London an impressive feat only some fifteen years after man precariously flew for the first time.

This aircraft had remarkable stability. On one occasion a V/1500 pilot suspected that his mechanic had neglected the fuel gauges. He left the controls to investigate. Suspicions were well founded; both the mechanic and his relief were asleep. But the V/1500's stability was undisturbed during the pilot's absence from the controls. On another occasion, when flying from Belfast to Folkestone, the same pilot left the controls for four minutes while he inspected the aircraft; no mishap occurred.

BERLIN BOMBER
From bases in England, big V/1500s were ready to bomb Berlin when the Great War ended. They were able to fly non-stop for twelve hours and were remarkably stable.

A GREAT FEAT
An impressive record was made by a four-engined V/1500 when it carried these forty passengers on a flight over London in 1919. They are seen, on the facing page, airborne over Westminster.

Ailerons, whose total surface exceeded an ordinary scout's wing-area, were balanced throughout their Length. A failure of both engines on one side did not impair stability and imposed no strain on the pilot.

Each of the four landing-wheels was 5 feet in diameter and the undercarriage was both simple and strong; in consequence the V/1500 could take-off from, and land on, uneven surfaces which wrecked smaller aircraft.

Petrol tanks contained 2½ gallons of fuel for each unit pound of weight, a higher ratio than was usual.

A radical departure in design was the absence of engine cowlings. Although abandoning the streamline principle in this respect, the designers saved the 500 lb weight of metal cowlings, made the engines more accessible for adjustment and repair and allowed a reduction in the size and weight of radiators.

A foretaste of the production methods which were to obtain during the World War was seen when some of the Handley Page 1914-18 aircraft were constructed to the parent concern's drawings by several companies in Britain and in quantity in the United States. Securing the co-operation of other organisations in manufacturing its aircraft has been a most successful feature of the Handley Page Company when war demands extreme quantity production.

Big Bomber Achievements

Only in the closing stages of the Great War did the aeroplane begin to exert an independent influence on its course. Such incidents as the annihilation of the Turkish Seventh Army demonstrated the terrible potency of air power. A successful employment of the "super-Handleys" would have been one of the most significant episodes of the war; it would have emphasised thirty years ago that the aeroplane restores mobility to ground forces.

For all time, the name of Handley Page will be associated with the evolution of the aeroplane as an independent offensive weapon. Nearly one thousand bombers of Handley Page design were ordered during the 1914-18 conflict. Many participated in spectacular exploits.

While admiring present day achievements, it should not be forgotten that the first long-distance flights were made by standard Handley Page Service aircraft during the Great War. One, for instance, was the first to fly thirty years ago from England to Egypt, this being the first flight from the United Kingdom to any destination outside Europe.

Early in 1917, a Handley Page O/400 bomber flew from England to Mudros, the Aegean base Constantinople (and the German cruiser Goeben which had taken refuge in the Turkish capital's harbour), Adrianople and other Turkish and Bulgarian towns.

When it is recalled that the world's first long-distance bombing raid — the attack on Constantinople — entailed a flight of 440 miles, mostly over sea and hostile country and through adverse weather, the significance of this exploit is realised. Only the twin-engined O/400 could carry enough fuel for the six-hour flight.

Aircraft were in so great a demand on the western front during most of the war that the full weight of the new arm could not be thrown into the scales of battle elsewhere.

However, in the later stages, another O/400 was released for service in the Near East. It flew to Palestine in the summer of 1918 and in time for General Allenby's offensive against the Turks' Jerusalem-Jaffa line. One vital contribution which the

TERRORISING THE TURKS
A Handley Page O/400 bomber in 1917 flew 440 miles to raid Constantinople and the German cruiser Goeben sheltering in the Turkish harbour.

KINGLY PRAISE
King George V inspects the O/400's cockpit. Germany, U-boat lairs along the Belgian coast and Turkish and Bulgarian targets in the East were attacked by Handley Pages during the Great War.

"ONE OF OURS"
Indian troops watch a Handley Page O/400 land during the Great War. On the Eastern Front, these big bombers made a vital contribution to the Allies' offensive effort; often merely their presence in the sky demoralised the enemy.

Handley Page bomber made to this engagement was the destruction, on the great battle's eve, of the Turkish GHQ's telegraph and telephone exchange.

Earlier, at the request of Colonel Lawrence (of Arabia), the O/400 had been sent to co-operate with Arab forces and, in addition to the valuable offensive work which it was able to do, the mere sight of this great aircraft soaring above their heads greatly energised Britain's allies while demoralising its enemies.

Following upon the Armistice and mindful, even at this period, of the importance of Imperial air communications, Major-General Sir Geoffrey Salmond, in command of the air forces in the Near East, made a pioneer flight in an O/400 from Cairo across the desert to Damascus and Baghdad, on to Karachi and then across India to Calcutta. With him went the present Air Vice-Marshal A. E. Borton, the late Captain Sir Ross Smith and two mechanics.

In the meantime, the Afghan war had begun. Military authorities tested the efficiency of the Berlin Bomber on a different objective — Kabul.

A V/1500 had followed the O/400 to India. Two notable non-stop legs were flown en route, the first over the 1,050 miles of sea from Malta to Egypt and the second across the 850 miles of desert from Cairo to Baghdad.

LONDON PRIDE
Londoners from 1915 onwards were cheered by the sight of their mighty bombers. An O/400 is framed in the arch at Hyde Park Corner en route to its operational base at Dukirk.

GOING ABOARD
King George V enters the Handley Page O/400 bomber in which his sons, now King George VI and the Duke of Windsor, made their first cross-channel flight in 1918.

However, it was feared that the V/1500, laden with bombs, would not climb above the mountains along the frontier on its way to the Afghan capital. Sir Geoffrey Salmond's O/400 was commissioned for the attack instead. Picketed in the open during its northward flight, however, it was destroyed in a cyclone.

If the raid were to be made, only the V/1500 was available and capable of the feat. It is a tribute to the big bomber that the mountains were crossed and re-crossed and the attack on Kabul accomplished with decisive effect.

ANCIENT AND MODERN
More than thirty years ago, Air Vice-Marshal A. E. Borton made the first England-Egypt flight. This was also the first flight from the United Kingdom to any destination outside Europe. He compares the O/400, in which he made his historic flight, with the new Handley Page Hermes. From the Aegean base, the Great War bomber made long-distance raids over enemy land and sea in operations against the Turks, Bulgarians and German naval forces.

TO INDIA IN 1918
A V/1500 followed an O/400 to India in 1918. En route it flew two notable non-stop legs: the 1,050 miles of sea from Malta to Egypt and the 850 miles of desert from Cairo to Baghdad.

BOMBS FOR KABUL
This V/1500 flew on to settle the Afghan war. It crossed the frontier mountains, bombed Kabul and returned safely to India.

Pioneering Air Travel

Military aircraft manufacture almost ceased at the end of the Great War and the Handley Page effort was directed into civil spheres.

Hostilities in 1914 had confronted a feeble British aircraft industry with the tremendous task of converting the sport of a few enthusiasts into a weapon of war. In four years, success had been attained.

When war ended, a big problem had to be faced and solved: the conversion of this powerful military arm into a social service. Promotion of air transport undertakings was a hazardous venture for unaided private enterprise. It was unassured of widespread public demand for air travel, it was in competition with highly-organised surface communications and it lacked the elaborate ground organisation which is essential to safe and reliable airline operation.

Nevertheless, the growing importance of speed in the commercial and social life of the post-war era gave assurance that an operational sphere existed for a medium which at least was twice as fast as surface travel.

To supply this need, no concern was better equipped than the Handley Page organisation. Having pioneered the big bomber during the war, the Company knew that those characteristics which enables an aeroplane to transport a great load of bombs are scarcely less efficacious when the carriage of an equal load of passengers or merchandise is required.

This had been proved by the RAF's No. 86 Communication Wing which operated His Majesty's Air Liner "Silver Star", a converted O/400. It was the first aeroplane to be used on a cross-Channel service, having been equipped to carry six passengers at the time of the Peace Conference in Paris to which it flew with the chief delegates. This former bomber's other distinction was that of being the first aircraft to undertake a night passenger service to France. For its initial efforts in civil aviation, Handley Page employed the twin-engined O/400 which had achieved such efficient service in day and night bombing during the Great War. Reserved for long-distance flights was its giant four-engined V/1500 super-bomber.

CRICKLEWOOD AIRPORT
Three of Handley Page Transport's airliner fleet at Cricklewood Airport in 1919. Converted from the Great War's famous O/400 bombers, they inaugurated Britain's overseas airline service.

TO PARIS
A Handley Page O/400 airliner of thirty years ago takes-off for the Continent.

CRADLE OF THE BIG AEROPLANE
Handley Page's Cricklewood works and aerodrome looked like this from a circuiting O/400 at the end of the Great War.

Founded in June, 1919, Handley Page Transport Ltd., inaugurated one of Britain's first commercial air transport services. An airline to Paris was instituted from Cricklewood aerodrome as soon as the official prohibition on civil flying was removed.

This London — Paris service, which started in August, 1919, was followed within a month by one to Brussels. Each operated daily in both directions. The establishment in November, 1919, of an official British air mail service between London and Paris supported the venture.

Operations were consolidated and extended in the summer of 1920, a line from London to Amsterdam being started.

Even at this early stage of civil aviation, the operational efficiency of the Handley Page service between London Paris and London — Amsterdam was 76% and 84% respectively. During this period, Handley Page Transport carried the majority of passengers on these routes. It was the sole operator to and from Brussels and its operational efficiency was as high as 94% .

Pilots who flew with Handley Page Transport in the early days included the present Marshal of the RAF, Lord Douglas, now Chairman of the British European Airways Corporation, and the late Air Commodore H. G. Brackley, Chief Executive of the British South American Airways Corporation.

Aeronautical development branched into two different spheres, military and commercial. Handley Page technicians were as successful in designing large commercial aeroplanes as they had been in the military sphere.

For the time, the airliner and bomber were basically the same aircraft. But between them the gap was increased and today the commercial aircraft is a specialised type as is the bomber. Handley Page was the first aircraft-construction company in the world to give definition to the two types.

Its first move in this direction was its new type of aircraft developed for these early airlines. It was the twin-engined W/8, a twelve-seater commercial biplane which gained easily the highest award in the Air Ministry's civil aviation competition in 1920 and set the seal on real luxury air travel. Later, at the International Meeting in Brussels, the Handley Page W/8 was awarded first prize for commercial aircraft.

For many years the holder of the World's record for weight-lifting, this new airliner was more powerful than its predecessor with Handley Page Transport, the O/700, a civil version of the O/400 bomber.

Economic difficulties began to hamper the airline services towards the end of 1920. Earlier, the Company which, with Handley Page Transport, pioneered the London-Paris services, had ceased to function. Another had started a sporadic service. For these British airlines, the situation became intolerable when official subsidies were granted to two French concerns which started services. Handley Page Transport, facing this heavily-subsidised foreign competition which involved severe cuts in fares and freight

FROM WAR TO PEACE

Earliest Handley Page airliners were converted from famous Great War bombers. H.M. Air Liner "Silver Star" (2), an O/400, flew statesmen from Britain to the Paris Peace Conference. This twin-engined type, as the O/700 (4), was given additional windows and an improved interior layout for its airliner role with Handley Page Transport Ltd. It is seen (3) with wings folded, a unique feature from the hangar-storage aspect. Reserved for long-distance flights was the giant 4-engined V/1500 (1) with its 126 ft wing-span and 40-passenger capacity which created a record.

rates, had to cease operations (although enthusiastic pilots had offered to continue flying without remuneration) until some official British support was forthcoming. Urged by public opinion and a vigorous Press campaign the British Government, because of French action, was obliged to subsidise air-transport in its turn. As a result of official guarantees, embodied in a provisional scheme of subsidy, Handley Page Transport recommenced its services after an interruption of less than three weeks.

Despite some improvement in the situation, the amount of traffic available proved to be insufficient to enable operation to be continued profitably, in view of the subsidised competition which obtained.

Co-operation between the British companies (three, by this time) was substituted for the rivalry which had existed hitherto. Handley Page Transport, as the leading British undertaking, received the important London — Paris service as its share of the traffic.

This line was extended some years later to Basle and Zurich and Handley Page Transport, therefore, had the honour of starting the Anglo-Swiss service. Three return trips were completed each week during the summer and one in winter.

PATHFINDER

Large Handley Page airliners were dominant in Britain's early commercial aviation. Flying many thousands of hours, they comprised a major part of Imperial Airways' fleet and consisted of W/8b's (5), a Hamilton (2), a Hampstead (1) and W/10's (3). They were developments of the W/8 (4). This 12-seater biplane had been operated by Handley Page Transport on its initial airline services to the Continent after winning the Air Ministry Civil Aviation Competition in 1920 and first prize at the International Meeting in Brussels for commercial aircraft.

From the beginning, Handley Page Transport's airliners achieved a higher commercial rendering than any others. In the year following March, 1920, 1,753 passengers were carried. During 1922, they had 4,008 passengers in all. Per trip, the average number was 5.81 in Handley Page aircraft; the best figure by a competitor was 2.95. This was an early indication of the payload qualities of Handley Page aircraft. In 1923, 7,146 passengers were carried, the average per aircraft having risen to 8.13. Each airliner which was operated by Handley Page Transport had a seating capacity of fourteen apart from one aircraft which was a ten-seater.

During this period of expansion and consolidation, the British Government decided that public funds should not be dispersed to competitive undertakings.

A monopolistic combine was created. In it each of the British air-transport companies — then numbering four — participated. Handley Page Transport Ltd. merged its identity in that of Imperial Airways in 1924. It was the nucleus around which the Corporation was built and, from these beginnings, the British Overseas and European Airways Corporations have evolved.

Handley Page airliners, after the merger, continued to occupy the same dominant

AIRBORNE COMFORT
Fast progress in early airliner cabins is seen when comparison is made between interiors of H.M.
Air Liner "Silver Star" (2), the HP O/400 used by Britain's delegates to the Paris Peace Conference
immediately after the Great War, the braced HP O/700 (3) which pioneered Handley Page Transport's
overseas airline routes in 1919, and the HP W/10 (1 and 4) of Imperial Airways whose nucleus, on
formation was the Handley Page operating company.

position in British commercial aviation as previously. They constituted the greater
part of the Imperial Airways' fleet.

Fourteen aircraft were operated by the new combine shortly after its inception.
Nine of them were Handley Pages. Three were twin-engined W/8b's produced in 1923,
one was a three-engined W/8f (Hamilton) of 1924 vintage, one a W/9 (Hampstead)
which was built in 1925 — and, in addition to more conventional service, was used
in New Guinea for transporting gold across jungle country which made no other
method possible — and four were twin-engined W/10's, constructed during 1926.

Their seating capacity indicates the even more striking Handley Page predominance.
Of Imperial Airways' total of 178 airliner seats, no less than 124 were provided by the
large 12-16-passenger Handley Page aircraft. A tribute to their efficiency were the
many thousand hours which each aeroplane flew.

Even in other countries, Handley Page airliners won approval by sheer merit despite
the usual obligation of subsidised undertakings to patronise only domestic products.
One example was the employment by SABENA, the Belgian operating company,
of Handley Page three-engined Hamilton airliners in the difficult conditions of the
Congo service. In this tropical region the Hamiltons operated with 100 per cent
reliability.

These airliners capable of 103 mph, were developments of the Air Ministry prize-
winning W/8. Other Handley Page aircraft inspired by the same theme were the

PARIS, BRUSSELS AND NEW YORK
Handley Page Transport's London — Paris service, which started in August 1919, was followed within a month by one to Brussels. A V/1500 is seen after landing at Brussels (1 and 2) and an O/700 on its arrival in Paris (3). Handley page aircraft made their way to the United States. Two lorry-loads of express-freight is seen being loaded (4) into a big V/1500 for the first Airplane Service of the American Railway Express Company prior to non-stop flight between New York and Chicago.

W/10 fleet which was produced for service with Imperial Airways. Each carried sixteen passengers. All were biplanes and this, apart from the 1926 three-engined Hamlet monoplane, was the design form for all Handley Page commercial aircraft until the modern Hermes made its advent after the World War.

Vindicated by years of operational experience was the contention which had been held by Handley Page Limited from the beginning that the success of airline operation was with the large, multi-engined aircraft which it had developed.

Aeronautical Panacea

Handley Pages's most important contribution to the progress of aviation, and ranking in importance side-by-side with its development of large-type aircraft, is its invention in 1919 and subsequent development of the slotted-wing. It is traced from early experiments in stability and control associated with the Company's first aircraft.

This slot discovery has been hailed throughout the world as the greatest achievement in the realm of aeronautics since man first conquered the air.

Fundamentally, the Handley Page slot increases the lift of a wing to which it is attached by allowing the wing to be flown at larger angles with consequent increase in speed range; in addition, it enables aircraft to be controlled at low flying speeds and to be free from spinning.

Today, the slot is used in order to increase the air-safety of the fast and heavily-loaded monoplane. For, with the increased wing-loading which is demanded with modern aircraft, the slot has become more and more important as an aid to widening the speed range and for the improvement of stability with consequent increase of safety.

In 1928, the Air Ministry ordered that Handley Page slots should be fitted to all British Service aircraft. This action resulted in the saving of many lives. Fatal accidents immediately decreased, being only 3.7 against 6.33 for the months of the preceding year. The stall-and-spin type of crash, a result of faulty manoeuvre, was eliminated. In the year before slots were fitted, there were 85 fatalities and 54 aircraft accidents; with slots in use, there were 42 fatalities and 31 aircraft accidents, despite more than a hundred additional front-line aircraft being in operation with a corresponding increase in the number of trainers.

Meanwhile, the slot was fitted to many types of light aeroplane and an immediate increase in the popularity of amateur flying can be traced to the greater safety and confidence which resulted.

Large commercial aircraft, including flying boats, also were equipped with slots. Imperial Airways ordered that all its aircraft were to be so fitted.

FIRST SLOTS
Early slotted-wing experiments were conducted on the HP 17, a DH9 biplane. It first flew with wing slots in 1920. Trials continued on the HP20 (*below*). A cantilever monoplane which was fitted with slots. It had a DH9A fuselage.

IMMORTALITY

Handley Page's fully-slotted and flapped Gugnunc biplane, a remarkable exponent of safe flight, was presented to the British Science Museum at South Kensington. There are preserved in honoured juxtaposition not only this, the first aircraft to fully demonstrate the possibilities of speed range extension by the use of slots and flap, but also a replica of the famous Wright aeroplane, first in the world to make a power-driven controlled flight.

GOING UP

Powers of the automatic interconnected wing-slots and flaps were demonstrated to the world twenty years ago by the flying qualities of the HP Gugnunc. It took-off in 80 yards and landed in 21 yards; its speed range was between 33½ and 112½ mph.

SHAKESPEARIAN SLOTS

A six-seater monoplane, the 1926 HP Hamlet had an enclosed cabin and was fitted with full-span slots. Originally it was twin-engined; a later version had three engines. This was the only non-biplane commercial aircraft to be built by Handley Page prior to the modern Hermes.

PRE-MUNICH UMBRELLA
With his umbrella used as a pointer, Lord Templewood (then Sir Samuel Hoare, Secretary of State for Air) is briefed on the Handley Page automatic wing slots.

SLOTS AND FLAPS
A Polish RWD6 demonstrates the potentialities of slots and flaps in the International Touring Competition of 1932.

SLOTS FOR EVEREST
Wing slots were part of the equipment of the Westland Wallace which was used on the pre-war Mount Everest air expedition.

Slots had world-wide application. By arrangement with Handley Page Ltd., they have been incorporated in aircraft built in no less than forty-three countries. Practically every important government has acquired for its nationals either the patents or the right to use the Handley Page slots.

So renowned has the slot become that a police constable, giving evidence in court, stated that a defendant, accused of being drunk in charge of a car, had said he was "well slotted". When the magistrate asked what was meant by this expression, he was told "stable in all directions sir, and under full control". Revenues from the slotted wing patents have amounted to approximately £750,000, mostly from foreign countries.

In the years during which the British aircraft industry tried to subsist on orders far too small to ensure healthy conditions, the returns from the slotted-wing invention was responsible, in large measure, for keeping the Company afloat and ready to meet the vital needs of the nation when RAF expansion was launched in 1935 as counter to German aggressiveness.

World attention was re-focused on the air-safety value of slots by the Guggenheim competition held in the United States in 1931 for aircraft which satisfied certain

STORCH'S SECRET
Excellent slow-flying capabilities of the Fieseler Storch are due to the application of Handley Page fixed slots which extend along the full span of its leading-edge together with flaps from the ailerons to the fuselage. It lands in a length no greater than its wing-span, yet has a maximum speed of 120 mph.

stringent tests as to safety and efficiency. Requirements were a minimum top speed of 110 mph, a slow speed of 35 mph, a climb of 400 feet per minute at 1,000 feet and the capacity to land in 100 feet and to take-off in 300 feet.

There were twenty-seven entrants. Only two aircraft survived the tests and both were slotted. One, a Handley Page biplane, was known as the Gugnunc. It had an incredibly steep angle of take-off, a top speed of 112½ mph and a minimum speed of 33½ mph. In a wind of 8 mph it could land and stop 63 feet after touching the ground. It could take-off in 240 feet.

Merits of the Gugnunc, which is preserved at the Science Museum in South Kensington, were not taken seriously in official quarters. But had the aircraft's latent possibilities been appreciated more widely, far greater speed in flying and far greater safety in landing would have been achieved earlier than they were.

SLOTS FOR THE ARMY
In the Lysander, automatic slots produced a spin-proof aeroplane withthe desired low minimum flying speed. It could be flown with marked carelessness yet with the utmost safety.

AMERICAN TAKE-OFF
A Curtiss Hawk fighter shows it excellent angle of climb after take-off. This was one of the first applications of Handley Page slots to United States aircraft.

War Planes in Demand Again

Military aircraft which came from the Handley Page works after the Great War confirmed the Company's proprietary association with the big bomber.

No attempt was made to continue the development of sheer size. Handley Page designers concentrated on the production of aircraft which embodied the best compromise between all factors conditioning the military aircraft's efficiency. In the immediate post-war years, an increase in the aeroplane's load-carrying capacity was not effected at the expense, for instance, of speed, rate-of-climb and service-ceiling improvements. Handley Page's Hyderabad bomber of this period, with certain exceptions necessitated by its military application, followed closely upon the lines of the famous W/8 which, in its various civil versions had proved to be of extremely high performance for its vintage and of very robust design and construction.

With a maximum speed of 109 mph, the Hyderabad carried a military load of 3,020 lb, it climbed at 800 fpm in comparison with the O/400's 340 fpm, and had a service ceiling of 14,000 feet against the O/400's 8,600 feet.

Thus the Hyderabad's increase of engine-power above that of the O/400 had been utilised to make but a relatively slight improvement in military load but achieved a substantial increase in speed, greatly raised the service-ceiling and more than doubled the climbing-rate.

This was the first large aircraft to use the Handley Page slotted-wing equipment. It had automatic wing-tip slots on the outer portions of the upper wings. These gave a high degree of lateral stability and the pilot had powerful and well-maintained control throughout the speed range.

On this aircraft was performed much of the development work of the automatic slot which relieves the pilot from any responsibility for correct opening and closing of the slots. These, between the auxiliary wing-tips and the main wings, open and close to the necessary extent under the air forces acting on them. Results which were obtained from the Hyderabad development work were of fundamental importance in the application of slots to large aeroplanes.

LAST WOODEN BOMBER
Similar in many respects to the famous HP W/8, the 1923 Hyderabad was the last Handley Page bomber of wooden construction. It was the first big aircraft to be fitted with automatic slots.

SLOTTED TORPEDO-CARRIER
The Hanley, a torpedo-carrier, was the first Handley Page aircraft designed for the application of slots. It first flew in 1922.

Various shipborne torpedo-carriers, bombers and fighters, reconnaissance day-bombers and troop-carriers also were built during this post-war period by the Handley Page organisation.

They included the 1922 Hanley, a single-engined torpedo-carrier which was the first Handley Page aircraft designed for slots; HP 21s, fully-slotted and flapped shipboard fighters which were built for the United States Navy in 1923; the Hendon torpedo-carrier which, fully slotted, was supplied in quantity to the RAF in 1924 and was the world's first aeroplane to land over the bow of an aircraft carrier in 1927; the Handcross day-bomber in 1924; and, two years later, the Harrow torpedo-carrier which, when fitted with a float undercarriage, became the first slotted seaplane.

Handley Page changed its form of construction from wood to metal in 1929.

Its first example was the Hinaidi night-bomber which was produced, as was the Hyderabad, in series for the RAF In every other way similar to its forebear, apart from engines, the Hinaidi with extreme power of manoeuvre, a low landing-speed and quick take-off qualities had extremely successful service with the RAF as did the Hyderabad.

Some of the Hinaidi's most spectacular active service operations were its rescue missions of the British Minister and civil population in the evacuation carried out by the RAF from Kabul at the end of 1928 during the Afghanistan civil war. It is an interesting link that an HP V/1500 bombed Kabul in 1919 and, some ten years later, another Handley Page aircraft helped to accomplish life-saving operations from the Afghan capital.

It was Hinaidi J7745 which had one of the most remarkable service records of any RAF aircraft. In India it had been kept largely in the open with temperatures of anything from 2° to 120° Fahrenheit. During the Kabul evacuations, it carried thirty-eight refugees and 11,200 lb of kit in eight journeys. When taking-off from Kabul, 6,400 feet above sea level, the maximum load was 11,570 lb. Take-off run, in these conditions, was 500 yards yet, in the words of the pilot, "once in the air, we climbed like a scout; we could have taken another 1,000 lb with ease".

This Hinaidi's most spectacular flight was that made from Bushire to Karachi. In twelve hours, 1,100 miles were covered. Having started before sunrise, it reached Karachi two hours after sunset. Not being equipped for night flying, it had a lighted stable lantern hanging from the cross-bracing wires in the fuselage. A difficult aircraft from the designers' point of view is the day-bomber. It must possess the qualities of all other military aircraft. Weight must be carried as for a night-bomber; it must have the same good all-round visibility and gun positions as for a general-purpose aircraft; it must perform and manoeuvre as does a single-seat fighter.

Hare, Handley Page's single-engined reconnaissance day-bomber, built in 1928 and with a speed of 145 mph, combined in an especially high degree the three important qualities of performance, manoeuvre and serviceability.

A NAVAL RECORD
The 1924 HP Hendon was the world's first aeroplane to land over the bow of an aircraft carrier.

TWO IN ONE
Handley Page's Handcross day-bomber in 1924 combined the manoeuvrability of the fighter with excellent load-carrying qualities.

TEN YEARS EARLY
During the 'thirties, many warplanes used Handley Page slots and wing flaps. A decade earlier, HP 21s, single-seat shipboard fighters were built for the United States Navy. They were fully slotted and flapped.

FIRST SLOTTED SEAPLANE
A third torpedo-carrier, the Harrow, was produced by Handley Page in 1926. When fitted with floats, it was the first slotted seaplane.

KABUL RESCUE
First sample of Handley Page's metal construction was the Hinaidi night-bomber for the RAF. No.
J.7745 played its part in the rescue operations during the Afghanistan civil war. Together with another
Hinaidi (*below*) it is seen loading evacuees at Kabul.

Handley Page next turned its attention, in the military sphere, to a multi-purpose,
well-armed heavy transport which was called Clive after the famous English soldier
and statesman who established British power in India. It was a result of the good work
performed by Hinaidis that this new aircraft was ordered by the RAF for work in India.

It was designed to fulfil any of five different functions: troop, freight or petrol carrier,
bomber or ambulance. Its various loads are interesting in comparison with those of the
Hastings, the Handley Page military transport of the present-day. As a troop carrier the
Clive transported seventeen fully-armed infantry men; as a freighter it lifted three large
engines; 400 gallons was its load as a petrol carrier; as a bomber it carried 1,300 lb for a
range of 765 miles; ten wounded (two being on stretchers) was its total complement in

SHOW PIECE

A Clive, operated by Sir Alan Cobham, was used for the pre-war National Aviation Day displays which included pull-off parachute descents. It carried more than a thousand passengers in one day.

INDIAN SERVICE

Handley Page produced the multi-purpose, heavy transport Clive in 1928. It functioned in India as a bomber, freighter and ambulance.

the ambulance role. The Clive, built in wood, dates from 1928; all-metal types followed in 1930. Their design was based on the lessons which were learned from the RAF's extensive experience with the Hinaidi, especially in connection with the Kabul rescue operations.

Sir Alan Cobham, in 1932, used the wooden Clive for his National Aviation Day displays. In 1933, the aircraft flew for 242 hours and carried 23,945 passengers. In one day, the Clive lifted 1,008 passengers, taking-off and landing forty-eight times.

BY NAME AND NATURE
A single engine reconnaissance day-bomber, the HP Hare was built in 1928. It had exceptional versatility in operational service.

World's First Real Airliner

Between the wars, Handley Page's most impressive achievements in airliner production were the Hannibal/Heracles class biplanes which first flew in 1930. For a decade, they made an outstanding contribution to commercial aviation.

They were the world's first four-engined air-transports. It was eight years later, for instance, before four-engined aircraft were introduced, as a great innovation, in the United States.

Handley Page's Hannibal class quickly earned the plaudits of the multitude; they were the world's most remarkable aeroplanes.

In design, they were hailed as daringly advanced. Previously no airliner so large and offering such spacious and luxurious passenger cabins had been produced. Hannibals were the first to break away entirely from the conception of the airliner as a modified war-time type and to be designed, complete with Pullman saloons, primarily for the passenger.

A fleet of eight aeroplanes of this HP 42 class, comprising the largest commercial airliners in regular use in any part of the world, went into Imperial Airways' service in 1931. Some 12,000 hours were registered by each of them and their aggregate mileage was upwards of 10 million.

Two forms of the HP 42 were built, the Eastern for operations in semi-tropical conditions on the long mail routes between Karachi, Cairo and Kisumu on the shores of Lake Victoria, and the Western for the London Continental service. Apart from interior arrangements, they were similar in every respect. Passenger accommodation in the Eastern type was less than in the Western in order that a big load of mails and freight could be carried.

They continued to prove their sterling qualities in airline operations up to the beginning of the World War when they were transferred to active-service transport duties with the RAF.

Setting a standard of safety, regularity and comfort previously unknown — and equal to, if not exceeding, that offered by surface transport — the Hannibals

HANNIBAL THE RENOWNED
From the advent of their operational service, the HP Hannibal/Heracles class airliners were supreme in commercial aviation.

established a tremendous reputation for efficiency and popularity with the world's travelling public.

Ample dimensions gave complete freedom of movement for every one of the forty passengers which each airliner carried. Travellers had a four-course hot lunch or seven-course hot dinner while they were being wafted to Paris and elsewhere. For seven years, these were the only airliners in which a full catering service was provided. From the fuselage, which was slung beneath the lower wings, passengers had an excellent outlook. Little noise reached the soundproofed cabins as quiet as within a train from the engines which were grouped closely together in nacelles on the top and bottom planes.

Smooth travel characterised the HP 42 class. An accelerometer recorded a maximum of 1.1 g in Helena on a trip to Paris. So stable was the airliner that, in bumpier air conditions
on the return to London, only a maximum of 1.39 g was recorded. This contrasts with 2.75 g registered in the coach trip from London to Croydon; in the French coach, true to the driving traditions of that nation, 4.75 g was recorded.

Although emphasis was on the luxury aspect of its passenger accommodation, the Hannibal class was designed for practical long-period service in the most arduous conditions. These airliners were easy to fly and to handle on the ground and to service, load and unload. They had a good take-off (in nine seconds) and docile short-distance landing at 50 mph.

Good-natured humorists talked about the Hannibal's "built-in headwinds"; they said it was as steady as the Rock of Gibraltar — and just as fast! In fact, the HP 42s for many years were the speediest aeroplanes for their payloads in existence. Their measured maximum speed was 136 mph and they had a speed range greater than any other airliner then in regular service. Before their advent, the Handley Page W/10s had been the fastest airliners in British service. Thus, the honour was kept in the family.

HP 42s were operated with an intensity which was superior not only to other types of aircraft but also to ships and railway trains. More than a thousand miles was the normal day's flying for an HP 42 in service, "turn-round" at the end of the journey being made in half an hour. This may be compared with the 650 miles which are steamed by a first-class ocean liner or the 350 miles covered by a railway locomotive. It is noteworthy that the crack express has a second train in reserve. No such standby was held on the services which were run by these Handley Page airliners.

They showed an economy of operation more than twice as good as that of the aeroplanes originally put into service on European airlines by Imperial Airways. Petrol consumption was 79 gallons an hour or about 46 miles per passenger per gallon. Their large capacity and low-running costs made possible a profit of more than £30 per working hour in ordinary conditions.

If 1925 be taken as the datum point and the capacity-ton-mile charges set at 100% for that year, in 1932, with the HP 42s in full operation, these charges had been cut to 49.6%. Insurance rates had been reduced substantially because of the safety of these airliners. Route mileage was six times greater.

Unequalled is the safety record of the Hannibal class. By virtue of their four engines being mounted closely together, there was consequent immunity from forced

BIGGER AND BETTER
First four-engined airliners in the world, HP 42s were also the most famous and popular during their decade of sterling service.

landings due to engine failure. These airliners were able to operate normally and with complete control on any combination of three engines. Captain A. Lamplugh, head of the British Aviation Insurance Co., writing to Handley Page Limited in 1937, said:

> "We have recently had before us statistics with regard to accidents to passengers travelling by specified types of aircraft operated by air transport services working to schedule. It may interest you to know that we cannot trace any serious injury to a passenger travelling in the 'Heracles' or 'Hannibal' types since these aircraft were brought into service some years ago. Furthermore, injuries to crew have been to all intents and purposes negligible.
> "You will appreciate that it is difficult to obtain statistics for various types of aircraft in use throughout the world, but it would appear to be reasonably certain that no other

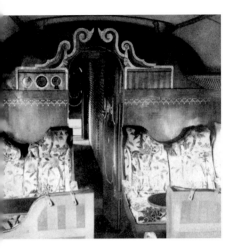

SETTING THE STANDARD
Keynote of the HP 42s interior was
spaciousness and comfort for it passengers
and crew. Travellers had an excellent view
from quiet cabins situated beneath the
wings and enjoyed a full catering service
during their smooth aerial progression.
These, nearly twenty years ago, were
unique features in civil aviation.

NO GREATER PRAISE
"Hannibal" circuits its Croydon base and
its temporarily groundborne relatives.
A dramatic critic of the time, writing
of a G. B. Shaw première at Malvern,
said "undoubtedly the pleasantest and
most memorable event of the day was
the journey to and from Malvern by the
airliner 'Heracles'".

single type has yet produced anything like such an excellent and continuous record of
safety to passengers."

In the history of air transport, nothing has had a more pronounced salutary effect
upon development generally and passenger traffic in particular than the introduction
of the HP 42 airliners. After a year's service, passengers on the London — Paris route
had increased by 119%. Giving statistics, the Air Ministry Resumé of Commercial
Information showed that in 1932, Imperial Airways, operating on the London —
Paris route, obtained a 98% increase in passengers carried as compared with the 15%
increase of the next best company operating over the same route. Commenting on
these figures, the Air Ministry Resumé stated:

> "The improved position of Imperial Airways, particularly so far as passenger traffic is
> concerned, must be largely attributed to the placing into service of the new Handley
> Page Heracles type aeroplane."

PYRAMIDS PIN-POINTED
Featured on Egyptian airmail stamps before the war was the HP Hannibal class.
This was a suitable tribute to the airliner's exceptional records of service in semi-tropical conditions on the long mail routes between Karachi, Cairo and Kisumu, near Lake Victoria.

SEEING FOR THEMSELVES
Most of the British Royal Family and many famous people travelled in the HP 42 airliners. The King (Duke of York at the time) and the late Duke and the Duchess of Kent are seen disembarking from the "Horatius" and "Heracles" respectively, at Croydon aerodrome.

Nearly half a million travellers, including most of the British Royal Family and many of the world's famous men, have travelled in HP 42 airliners on the European and Empire routes an which they functioned under Imperial Airways' banner. Once, in Glasgow, when the Heracles was introducing itself to the public prior to regular airline service, it carried three thousand people into the air in three days.

HP 42s were aeronautical history-makers in their long, safe service; the outcome of twenty-five years' experience, they were the safest, the most paying and the most comfortable airliners, in existence.

Eight years after they started operations, the Chairman of Imperial Airways, in a public commendation, said that the Hannibal class had a record of reliability and safety of which its designers and constructors well could be proud.

Earlier in 1934, Imperial Airways had congratulated the. Handley Page Company on its airliners having given continual satisfaction for thirteen years. They had established records by carrying more people, flying a greater mileage and operating with a greater margin of safety than any other aircraft throughout the world.

IMPERIAL AIRWAYS LTD.

TELEGRAMS IMPAIRLIM, LONDON
TELEPHONE VICTORIA 3211.

AIRWAY TERMINUS,
VICTORIA STATION,
LONDON, S.W.I.

12th May 1936.

Dear Mr. Handley Page,

I feel that I am fulfilling the wish of the Board in writing you a letter of appreciation of the good service given by the "Hanibal" and "Heracles" types of aircraft which your Company designed and built for us.

These eight aircraft have flown collectively about fifty two thousand hours, or five million miles, and have consistently fulfilled all the traffic demands made upon them. They have flown night and day in all weathers and in all climates and have maintained standards of regularity and comfort which we do not think have yet been excelled.

We still look forward with confidence to further useful work with these aircraft on the main line services whilst replacement aircraft we have ordered are being established, and thereafter on our ancillary and relief services.

They are indeed a credit to your great firm.

Yours sincerely,

CHAIRMAN.

F.Handley Page, Esq. C.B.E.
Handley Page Ltd.
Claremont Road,
CRICKLEWOOD,
N.W.2.

MILEAGE MILLIONAIRE FLEET
Its pilot boards the "Heracles" prior to flying it on its millionth air-mile. Imperial Airways' HP 42 fleet flew 100,000 hours and the aggregate mileage of these eight airliners was upwards of ten million in all conditions and climates of operational service.

Vital Years of Rearmament

For some time, it had been apparent that the big aeroplanes which Handley Page was building at Cricklewood had outgrown the airfield attached to the works. And so, the old flying-field became a housing estate and, in the early '30s, a new aerodrome was constructed by the Company at Radlett in Hertfordshire.

When the late Duke of Kent opened the new aerodrome, Sir Frederick Handley Page said, characteristically, that "between two ancient avenues of communication, Watling Street and the LMS Railway, the Company has its aerodrome which provides one of the avenues of communication for the future."

Well-equipped with modern assembly halls, hangars and running sheds, this aerodrome is complete with long tarmac and concrete runways and the other facilities which are required for test-flying large four-engined aircraft. For it is at Radlett that all Handley Page aircraft now are assembled and test-flown. There, too, experimental flying and research are undertaken and modern press shop is situated.

In 1933 the Heyford, a biplane night-bomber of all-metal frame construction, was put into production. It had a speed of 142 mph (earning for itself the adjective "express"), was well protected by three gun-turrets, giving the most intense field of fire devised up to that time, and carried a very large load of bombs for 2,000 miles.

In service with the RAF, having been judged during its official trials to be the most efficient biplane ever tested up to that time, this aircraft proved its merit; it was a good bomber, being a steady platform for aerial firing and eminently suitable for all kinds of formation flying. Still with the RAF at the beginning of the World War, it proved of extreme value as a navigational and gunnery trainer for embryo aircrews.

Up to this time, the bombers' formula had not altered drastically. But the Heyford showed a marked change and introduced many original features, including the rotating gun-turret which retracted into the fuselage when not in use. Another was the special design for easy and quick servicing.

A characteristic of these bombers, giving them a formidable air, was the positioning of fuselage and engine-nacelles close under the top plane. Improved aerodynamic

A FORMIDABLE AIR
Handley Page's Heyford night-bomber of 1933 was renowned for its hitting power and good all-round performance.

characteristics and crew visibility resulted. Mechanics were enabled to operate starting handles and refuelling systems with complete safety.

Although at this time retractable undercarriages were receiving much attention, the Heyford was fitted with a fixed type. Much thought had been given by the Handley Page design team to this point. By bringing the Heyford's undercarriage close under, and partly within, the lower plane, drag was reduced to such an extent that advantage for the Heyford was seen in the fixed undercarriage.

Special attention had been given to detailed design so that this new bomber could be constructed readily by quantity production methods. The jigging and tooling system which was used resulted in simple manufacturing processes. They increased the speed of production and, at the same time, permitted complete inter-changeability of parts between one Heyford and another.

Another torpedo-bomber, the HP 46, followed in 1932 and a general-purpose bomber and torpedo-carrier in 1935. This, the HP 47, was a low-wing metal monoplane.

Air Ministry having asked for an aircraft which could go anywhere and do anything, it got in this high-performance monoplane, an aeroplane which operated with equal efficiency in various climates and temperatures and was able to use all forms of aerodrome and temporary landing-field.

Its scope of military usage was greater than any earlier warplane and it applied the famed qualities of slots and flaps to the performance of its duties which included bombing, photography, reconnaissance, torpedo-carrying, ambulance work and even troop-carrying on a small scale. Never before exceeded, were the attributes of this aircraft both in landing and flying
qualities and in varied duties efficiently performed.

Earlier, the HP 43, a prototype three-engined bomber-transport, had been produced. Apart from the difference in the number of engines, it bore a marked resemblance to the Hannibal class airliners. This aircraft was converted into a twin-engined monoplane in 1935 and was re-styled the HP 51.

Quickly following came the Harrow, a big monoplane bomber which, at the time, was known as the "heavyweight champion of the world". It had a high performance, despite its greatly increased load-carrying ability in comparison with preceding types, and was a first-class example of all-round efficiency as comprising performance, ease of production, serviceability and robustness. With a range of 1,840 miles, and in spite of its girth, the Harrow had a speed of 200 mph and a service ceiling of 10,000 feet.

It made history almost as notable as the earlier Handley Page bombers by being the first new type of aircraft ordered under the RAF expansion scheme to come into production and reach the squadrons in series. In fact, the Harrow demonstrated fully the hitherto unrealised possibilities of correct production planning of military aircraft.

ROYAL REVIEW
Bigger now (with more assembly-halls and long, heavy-duty runways) is the Handley Page Radlett aerodrome than when opened in 1930. Then, the Handley Page types displayed on the perimeter included the Clive, Hinaidi, Hyderabad, Hamilton, Heyford and Hannibal.

WELL AND TRULY OPENED
The late Duke of Kent (when Prince George) opened Handley Page's new aerodrome at Radlett in Hertfordshire. It has every facility required for the assembly and air-testing of the Company's big, four-engined aeroplanes.

THREE KINGS
Under the nose of an HP Heyford are three Kings of England — George V, Edward VIII (then Prince of Wales) and George VI (Duke of York at the time).

DUSTBIN AMIDSHIPS
One of the Heyford's many original features was the rotating gun-turret which retracted into the fuselage when not in use. Its three turrets gave the greatest aerial fire-power devised up to that time.

MOST EFFICIENT BIPLANES
HP Heyfords were perfect aircraft for all kinds of formation flying. On official trials, this night-bomber was judged to be the most efficient biplane ever tested. Its long service with the RAF culminated in training duties during the World War.

ANOTHER ROYAL INSPECTION
The Duke of Windsor (then King Edward VIII) is
seen inspecting a squadron of Heyfords on another
occasion.

Aerodynamically, it was important by marking the heavy bomber's transition stage
from biplane to monoplane. It retained the fixed-undercarriage wings being mounted
high on the fuselage, the undercarriage was designed to offer a minimum resistance.
A consequent saving in weight offset any advantage which a retractable undercarriage
might have bestowed.

When the Harrows ceased to function as bombers, they were converted into
transports and, in this role, were employed throughout the World War. Their most
renowned part was played at Arnhem in the closing stages of hostilities. Being the only
large aircraft available and able to land and take-off from small fields, to the Harrow fell
the honour of evacuating British paratroops wounded during the Arnhem fighting.

Most advanced bombing aircraft in the world of its day, the all-metal Hampden,
which issued next from the Handley Page works, was designed specifically to fit it for
the fast-production requirements of the rearmament programme. Indicative of the
rapidity with which Handley Page bomber design had progressed was the Hampden's
ability to carry a bigger load over a longer distance and at a much higher speed than
the Harrow, although being much smaller.

With, at this time, the incredibly fast speed of 254 mph and extreme manoeuvrability, it
had a range of 1,460 miles, operational ceiling of 15,000 feet, and ability to carry a big load.

UBIQUITY
A low-wing metal monoplane, the slotted and flapped HP 47 was a 1935 answer to the British Air Ministry's plea for a high-performance aircraft which could go anywhere and do anything.

FIRST FOR THE RAF
The HP Harrow was the first new type of aircraft ordered under the RAF expansion scheme.

NEW LOOK

A close resemblance is seen between the Hannibal/Heracles airliners and the HP 43, a prototype 3-engined bomber-transport which was built in 1932. Converted into a twin-engined monoplane three years later, it was re-styled the HP 51.

HEAVYWEIGHT CHAMPIONS
HP Harrows in 1936 marked the heavy-bomber's transition from biplane to monoplane. Operationally, they had all-round efficiency and functioned throughout the war.

Like the Harrow, the Hampden embodied the most advanced wing-slot equipment. This enabled its very high top speed to be obtained without sacrificing a desirably low landing speed. In consequence, under active-service conditions, the Hampden proved easy to handle although its speed and rate of climb were greatly in advance of its contemporaries.

Squadrons of them were off the mark at once when hostilities commenced. They attacked all parts of Germany during the first years of the World War. In the later stages, they operated as Coastal Command torpedo-bombers and were used for parachute mine-laying.

Apart from being one of the most efficient aeroplanes in the world for sheer load-carrying capacity in relation to power and high speed, the Hampden proved to be most remarkable because of the reduction in man-hours involved in its production. This was consequent upon the split-construction and unit-assembly methods which were originated and developed by Handley Page and first introduced in part during the production of the Harrow bomber in 1936. This system was a model of production efficiency and genius; the world's aircraft constructors emulated the methods which were employed.

SPLIT-CONSTRUCTION
Designed for fast production by split-construction methods, the HP Harrow was the first aircraft
under the pre-war rearmament programme to be built in series and to reach the squadrons.

HIGH LEVEL PARADE
The King visited Handley Page at the end of 1937, and inspected a Harrow heavy-bomber squadron. He is accompanied by Marshal of the RAF, Lord Newall, then Chief of the Air Staff.

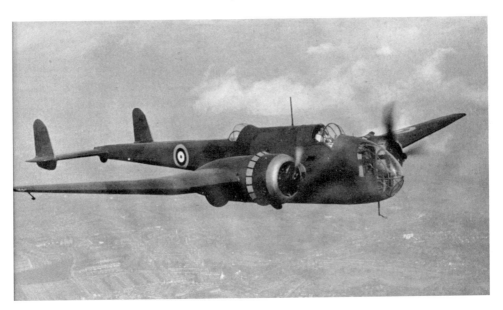

DEFENDER OF CIVIL LIBERTIES
Produced in order to strengthen Britain's hand against German aggressiveness, the high-performance
HP Hampden was well-named after the seventeenth-century opponent of all kinds of tyranny.

RECORD PRODUCTION
Handley Page's split-construction and unit-assembly methods have been developed in successive stages
firstly for large components and subsequently for smaller ones. Record production rates achieved with
the Hampden had been thought unobtainable previously.

"FLYING SUITCASES"

Although their fuselage shape inspired the appellation, it was a tribute to the high-performance Hampden bombers' compactness that they were know throughout the RAF as "flying suitcases".

Split-construction consists, essentially, in designing an aircraft in a much great number of parts than was possible or considered desirable with earlier wood and metal aircraft and, accurately timed in manufacture, bringing them together to form a complete component. Men are positioned for work so that each can do his job simultaneously and without getting in his fellows' way.

To aircraft, split-component production is what the conveyor system is to the motor-car. And in this way, Handley Page has brought its aircraft manufacturing technique as near as possible to the mass-production system. Such methods enabled the Hampdens and their in-line engined counterparts, the Herefords, to be turned out in series more rapidly than any other aircraft of similar type not only by Handley Page at Cricklewood but elsewhere in Britain and also in Canada.

War and the Halifax

Twenty-four years after Handley Page built the world's first big aircraft, the father of all modern heavy bombers, it produced the Halifax as a worthy lineal descendant of this parent.

But, though the O/100 was not conceived until after the beginning of the Great War, the Halifax was in the design stages almost three years before the World War began.

This is a measure of the air-weapon's recognition in official quarters. It is very positive evidence of the far-sighted policy of Britain's Air Staff which rightly came to the conclusion that, for any aerial offensive to be effective, great loads of bombs had to be transported and, therefore, aircraft of a large size were an essential need as equipment.

Thus, the Halifax was in the van of the offensive when in 1941 large scale air-warfare was switched from the Luftwaffe's attacks on Britain to the pounding of Germany by the RAF. Night after night, Bomber Command's Halifax squadrons took the war into Hitler's European Fortress and into Mussolini's Roman Empire. In those early days, the A.O.C. in C. of Bomber Command could report: "Halifaxes have attacked Germany and Italy during the past week in the heaviest raids ever made on Berlin and Turin. Their performance is excellent by night and by day. We cannot have too many Halifaxes."

Lord Halifax had foreshadowed its lethal powers when he christened the Halifax. Quoting an old Yorkshire prayer, "from Hull, Hell and Halifax, good Lord, deliver us", he foretold that the Germans might well use the same plea during the months and years which were to come.

Throughout the war, Halifaxes were in the forefront of the British aerial offensive. In all, more than 6,000 of them were produced, or more than 40 per cent of Britain's total heavy-bomber power.

In the bombing operations alone, approximately 76,000 sorties were flown and nearly a quarter of a million tons of bombs were dropped on to enemy targets.

ZERO HOUR
To the menacing roar of it five thousand horsepower, a veteran HP Halifax takes-off in the gloaming en route again to Hitler's Reich with a 6-ton bomb-load for express delivery.

Bomber Command had no less than seventy-six Halifax squadrons in action at the time of its peak strength.

One of the greatest characteristics which aircrews appreciated in the design and construction of the new heavy-bombers, of stressed skin construction, was their ability to withstand a great deal of damage from flak and gun-fire and yet to return safely to base.

Many tales of the "home-on-a-wing-and-a-prayer" variety might be told. A Halifax returned from Germany on one engine; another got back with its port fin and rudder shot away; a third returned with its front gun-turret and bomb-aimer's station blown-off and the crew almost frozen to death.

Many Halifax versions were produced from the prototype bomber for different combat roles as the Allied offensive developed. Halifaxes functioned as long-range reconnaissance and transport aircraft, as airborne-assault vehicles and glider-tugs.

Those of Bomber Command participated in every major raid on the Greater Reich and enemy-occupied territory. They were among the first aircraft to be employed in the Pathfinder Force. Apart from bombing, Halifaxes with the Command nightly laid mines in enemy waters. They flew Allied agents far into occupied territory and dropped arms to partisans.

Because of their great range, Halifaxes were of especial value for reconnaissance patrols with Coastal Command. Armed with depth-charges, they were a mainstay of the RAF's anti-U-boat action. Their operations, into the Atlantic on meteorological reconnaissance went on day after day, unceasingly in all weathers.

As glider-tug the Halifax did all the heavy work. It was the only aircraft which hauled into battle the Airborne Forces' giant tank-carrying glider. Alternatively, it carried eighteen fully-equipped paratroops and thirteen containers of arms and equipment to target areas behind the enemy lines.

Finally, the CVIII Halifax was produced as a military transport with its large pannier in place of the bomb-bay.

ARNHEM BOUND

A Halifax tows a heavy Hamilcar glider on its way to Arnhem. Halifaxes had the distinction of being the only tugs which hauled the Airborne Forces' big tank-carrying gliders into battle. In this operational sphere, the Halifax load was eighteen fully-equipped paratroops and thirteen large containers of arms.

It was not mere chance that, less than two months after the outbreak of war, the first Halifax commenced its flight trials. Years before, and initiated at Air Staff level, the strategic requirements of an air-offensive had been foreseen and laid down. And, two decades of Handley Page experience in big aircraft building had made possible the engineering expression of a military requirement.

HP 56, the original design, was to have two of the new 24-cylinder Rolls-Royce Vulture engines which were under development at the time. By the middle of 1937, however, the Air Ministry asked for the HP 56 to be re-designed in order to take four Rolls-Royce Merlins, as it was anticipated that not enough Vultures would be available to meet the demand which would be made on this engine for Britain's large-scale rearmament programme.

Many major modifications followed as the result of this change. Re-designated the HP 57, the basic design was unchanged, although wing-span and maximum weight increased.

It remained a mid-wing cantilever monoplane which was to be constructed throughout on the modern all-metal, stressed-skin principle and designed not only to carry a big bomb-load over long distances, but also to withstand the heavy damage likely to be inflicted upon it.

All in all, there was nothing very unorthodox about the design of the Halifax. And, although it had a wing-span of nearly 100 feet it did not look unduly large and certainly not disproportionate. In it, crew comfort reached a new high standard and, in particular, the new gun-turrets represented a great advance on the open turrets of earlier bombers.

Seven weeks after the outbreak of war, in 1939, and only twenty-two months after its construction began, the first Halifax prototype flew. It was found to be one of the finest aircraft structures ever built. In consequence of its low weight in relation to its size and horsepower, it proved to be one of the most efficient aircraft in the world.

Following upon the precedent established in the case of an earlier Handley Page heavy-bomber, the Harrow, the Halifax was put into production even before the prototype flew.

Little modification was needed and the "first off" flew in October, 1940. Within five weeks, the first Halifax squadron of Bomber Command was being formed, and, exactly five months after the first production aircraft flew, Halifaxes made their initial operational sorties against Kiel and Le Havre.

In service, the new bomber soon proved to be very popular. It had no vices and its operational performance marked a great advance on contemporary types.

Not only could this big aeroplane fly at 265 mph, but it had a maximum range of 3,000 miles and carried a bomb-load of nearly six tons. Take-off run was comparatively short, being only 1,020 yards, at a weight of 55,000 lb, or 1,250 yards at a weight of 58,000 lb in order to clear 50 feet. With full load, the initial rate of climb was 750 feet per minute, at a weight of 58,000 lb.

Later refinements and modifications to the aircraft resulted from the RAF's operational experience with the Halifax. They reflected upon the performance of the bomber which, in its Mark VI version with an all-up weight of 68,000 lb, had a cruising speed of 265 mph, service ceiling of 25,000 ft., and bomb-load of 6½ tons.

However, performance alone will not make an aircraft suitable for war operation. It must be capable of being produced simply and cheaply, must be of a robust construction so that maintenance man-hours are low and must be capable of a wide range of inter-changeability. Actually, the Halifax was one of the cheapest aircraft, for its size, produced during the war.

Its ease of production was ensured by the split-construction and unit-assembly methods which Handley Page had originated and developed. In order to simplify and accelerate Halifax production, the entire aeroplane was split up into some dozen major assemblies. This method not only enabled far more operators to work on each assembly stage, thus speeding output, but also facilitated transport and repair. In consequence the aeroplane could be put together very quickly and with a minimum of labour once the sub-assemblies had been completed.

One significant result of this production technique enabled Handley Page to mobilise the services of various engineering companies, many of them new to aircraft production, when the Air Ministry decided in 1940 to proceed with all-out Halifax construction. A manufacturing group of companies was established with Handley Page as the parent-concern. It was the first of the associations devoted to big bomber production.

An obvious choice was the first member of the Halifax production group. It was the English Electric Company, which already had won renown for its modern production

STURDY BOMBERS

Left: This Halifax had its nose removed in the air by the wing of another big bomber when the two aircraft collided. It returned to base and landed safely. *Right:* The King sees the damage received by a Halifax during a raid on Germany. Rugged Handley Page bombers are renowned for their ability to fly back to base despite the enemy's hostility.

methods while building HP Hampdens. Other companies brought into Halifax production were: Rootes, Securities, Fairey Aviation Co. Ltd., and the London Aircraft Production Group (which included the London Passenger Transport Board, Park Royal Coach Works, the Express Motor and Body Works, Chrysler Motors and Duple Bodies and Motors).

Each company having "dominion status", the parent-firm acted as consulting engineer for the group and tendered advice and help to all contractors with the object of bringing Halifax aircraft up to the highest possible standard. On the parent-firm rested the burden of proving the jigs, getting the manufacturing layout settled and placing all its experience at the disposal of the daughter-firms.

Thus, the Halifax group consisted of five companies of equal status from a manufacturing point of view with common problems in administrative and material supply, in manufacturing procedure and in contract-fulfilment conditions.

In order to maintain a high standard of aircraft production, one aircraft from each hundred produced by daughter-firms was flown to the Handley Page aerodrome and tested by the parentcompany's pilots. Any adjustments necessary were reported to the daughter-firms concerned.

Halifax production was speeded by using the photo-lofting technique, of which Handley Page is the pioneer in Britain. Components of the aircraft were drawn accurately on specially prepared metal sheets which subsequently were photographed. These drawings were then reproduced photographically on suitably sensitised metal

AN HP "SPEEDBIRD"
With the dearth of civilian transports at the end of the war, twelve Halifaxes were converted into fast Halton airliners for BOAC. They operated on the African and Indian routes and cut earlier journey times by more than a third.

sheets. Exact copies of the original design, they were circulated to the daughter-firms and sub-contractors in order to facilitate manufacture.

When large quantities of a particular component were required, it was from these reproductions that the appropriate tools for mass-production were made. When only small quantities were wanted, a photo-reproduction was made on the metal to be used in manufacture. This enabled it to be cut and shaped without prior marking-out in the shops or the construction of special tools.

As all reproductions were identical, so were all manufactured components. Thus complete inter-changeability was assured and "tailoring" was eliminated.

Main advantages of this technique were: the standardisation of all basic contours which did not vary; any number of exact copies of a drawing could be supplied to daughter-firms or subcontractors; reproduction could be on any material, thus facilitating the manufacture of jigs and templates or components; slightly enlarged reproductions could be made in order to simplify the manufacture of the drop-hammer dies used for forming complex shapes.

This technique, together with the Handley Page system of split-construction and unit-assembly, were the main factors behind the high rate of Halifax production.

Between 1940 and the middle of 1944, Halifaxes totalling 4,046 were contributed to the aggregate British bomber output, of 10,018 built. In all, 6,176 Halifaxes were produced. This group production was ten times the entire heavy bomber output in the Great War, and, an a weight basis, was forty-five times greater.

EXPRESS FREIGHT
Halifaxes are operating in the post-war civil-freighting sphere. They fly to all parts of the world with large payloads of diverse merchandise and have made an important contribution to the Berlin airlift.

During its period of peak production, the Halifax group comprised forty-one factories and dispersal units (7½ million square feet), 600 sub-contractors and 51,000 employees.

By it, one complete Halifax was produced each working hour. This involved 30,000 different components. In one hour, 256,000 airframe parts, excluding rivets, were made, fitted and inspected: two-thirds of an acre (7 tons) of light alloy sheet was cut, formed and fitted; three miles of sheet metal was rolled or drawn into sections; five miles of light alloy special extruded sections were cut, drilled and fitted; 700,000 rivets were closed; three to four miles of electric cable and one mile of pipes were fitted.

As operational requirements changed, so new tactics were developed. Halifaxes were modified in order to keep them in the forefront of battle.

All equipment necessary for day and night operations in any part of the world was incorporated in later Halifax bombers. More and more attention was being paid to preparations for the Asiatic war and "tropicalisation" was the prime need for all new types. Before the German surrender, several Halifax squadrons were sent to the East in order to operate against the Japanese. The advent of the atom-bomb prevented them attacking Nippon itself.

Halifaxes had been used operationally in overseas war zones earlier. Squadrons had been sent to Egypt in order to give heavy-bomber support to the newly-formed British Army of the Nile. They attacked the German Afrika Korps and its naval and air-supporting units from Alamein until the final surrender. Others were modified in order to carry in their bomb-bays such loads as Merlin engines. In this way, they helped to maintain the Desert Air Force's fighter-squadrons at 97 per cent operational strength during the fast-moving North African campaign.

Specialised versions of the Halifax went out of production only at the end of 1946. Chief reason for its longevity was its great versatility. It is a tribute to its original basic design that virtually it remained unchanged through twenty-six major variants which were produced to fit it for six different combat roles.

It had been apparent, during the middle of the war, that the Halifax not only was a first-rate bomber, but also that it had excellent potentialities as transport, freighter, ambulance and glider-tug. Several bomber versions had their guns, turrets and scanners removed and were otherwise modified in order to carry passengers, freight and stretchers.

So efficient did these Halifax transports prove to be that a special version, the Mk. CVIII, was produced. It carried no guns, the rear-turret was replaced by a fairing and additional port-holes and escape hatches were provided. Its most significant feature as a transport was the large, streamlined pannier, fitted to the underside of the fuselage. A usable volume of 272 cubic feet accommodated nearly four tons of freight.

Other Halifaxes were fitted with glider-towing hooks and other equipment thus suiting them to the needs of the Airborne Forces. In all airborne operations from Norway to Normandy, at Arnhem and in the last great operation of the Rhine crossing, these Airborne Forces' Halifaxes were used. They had no top turrets, but retained fore and aft guns. When really heavy gliders became available in quantity for the transport of small tanks and guns, Halifaxes were used to tow them. They had the distinction of being the only aircraft which were capable of towing these fully-loaded giant gliders. A special variant, for transporting the Airborne Forces' heavy-equipment, was adapted to carry, all in its bomb-bay, a jeep and a 6-pounder gun, complete with ammunition and accessories. These were dropped in the ordinary way by parachute and crews for the gun and jeep jumped from the aircraft's fuselage. Latest and last of the Airborne Forces' Halifaxes have a large paratroop door in the floor and two 0.5-in. guns in the rear turret.

Currently, the Halifax continues in Royal Air Force service as a fast, long-distance transport, as vehicle for airborne support, as meteorological reconnaissance aircraft over the Atlantic and as a long-distance training and liaison aeroplane.

Other Halifaxes are operated by the French Air Force. In addition to their purely military roles as bombers and meteorological reconnaissance aircraft, they fly civilian passenger services to several distant parts of the world including South America. These veteran bombers, operated by the French, have established a unique record by transporting no less than thirty-two people from France to West Africa per flight.

With the urgent need for non-military aircraft at the end of six war years, Halifaxes were pressed into general service as civil freighters and passenger transports.

A fleet was converted for the British Overseas Airways Corporation and, operating on the African and Indian routes, cut earlier journey times by more than a third. BOAC had been quick to appreciate the possibilities of the war-tried Halifax for commercial services.

Exhaustive flight tests were made on the 4,500-mile London — West African routes soon after the war ended. One "guinea-pig" Halifax flew for two months at the equivalent operating rate of 3,061 hours-a-year on these initial proving fights. Another participated at a utilisation-rate almost as high. Further tests, in view of this performance, were considered to be a waste of time. After conversion, the Halifax fleet was re-christened Halton and pressed into service.

BOAC had proved for itself (at 3.94 man-hours per flying hour) the low cost of Halifax maintenance — a feature which had become well-known to the RAF after years of operational experience with the aircraft. In its report on this factor, BOAC stated:

> "... this figure is most satisfactory and shows every indication of being far better in the case of the Halifax than any other four-engined aircraft now being used by the Corporation."

Other Halifaxes, as charter airliners, are crossing, the Atlantic from New York to London in fifteen hours.

In the civil freighting sphere. Halifaxes, operated by air-charter companies, have been flying to all parts of the world with 7-ton payloads of miscellaneous merchandise (fruit, textiles, bullion, radios, mails, etc.) packed in the fuselage and commodious pannier of each aircraft. One made a round-the-world "tramping" flight of 27,000 miles and broke several flying records en route. Others have distinguished themselves by transporting to various parts of the world heavy and Cumbersome spares for disabled ships, thereby saving the heavy costs which would have been incurred by the merchantmen's continued immobility.

Halifaxes, operating as civil freighters, played an important part in beating the Berlin blockade. A typical Halifax load of basic needs for the German capital was 6½ tons. Some of these former warplanes, for which the Berlin run was not a novelty, were converted to air-tankers and carried diesel-oil. An ordinary lorry tank was fitted in place of the usual pannier beneath the fuselage and on each trip a cargo of 1,500 gallons of oil carried.

In the Halifax, Handley Page's new military and civil aircraft have a fine example before them. Their flying characteristics to date indicate that they will be worthy of the Halifax tradition and of a pedigree which has been well-defined during the last forty years.

QUALITY WITH QUANTITY

Above: One of the final-assembly lines at the Handley Page works when the Halifax output was being geared up to its maximum of a bomber an hour. *Right:* Already joined, the centre and rear sections of a Halifax await their nose assembly. Group production of this bomber during the World War involved 600 subcontractors and 51,000 employees.

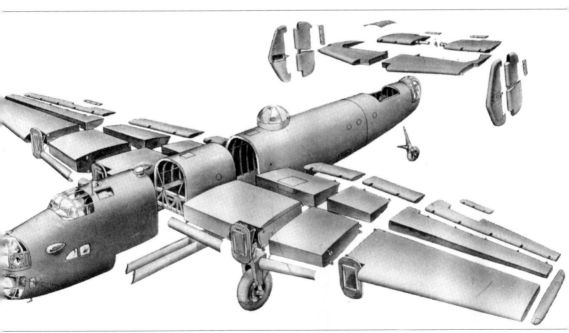

BITS AND PIECES

By splitting the Halifax into major sections, each suitable for production at small factories, a gargantuan output was achieved. More than 6,000 were built — more than forty per cent of Britain's war-time heavy-bomber strength.

HALIFAX BI
Heavy bomber powered by four Merlin X engines; 2-gun front and 4-gun rear turret; some had beam guns; all-up weight 55,000 lb. Series II bombers of this mark stressed for 60,000 lb; Series III had increased tankage.

HALIFAX BII SERIES I
Similar to BI Series III except for Merlin XX or XXII engines, addition of 2-gun Hudson top turret and removal of beam-guns. Had additional tankage and all-up weight of 60,000 lb.

HALIFAX BII SERIES IA
Similar to BII Series I (Special) apart from perspex nose, with one gun, and square fins fitted to some bombers.

HALIFAX BII SERIES I (SPECIAL)
Similar to BII Series I. Front turret replaced by fairing; Defiant 4-gun top-turret normally fitted; 60,000 lb all-up weight.

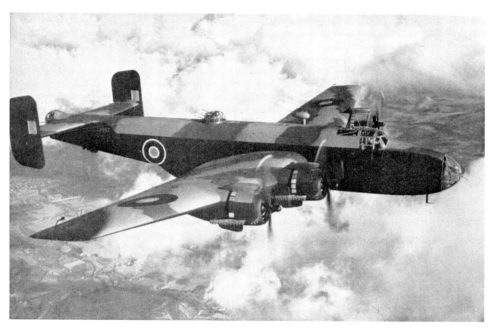

HALIFAX BIII
Generally similar to BII Series IA; Hercules XVI engines; scanner and 0.5-inch gun-turret; retractable tail-wheel; extended wing-tips for some; all-up weight increased to 65,000 lb. BIV was an experimental aircraft; BVs similar to BIIs apart from different undercarriages and propellers.

HALIFAX BVI
Similar to BIII. Hercules 100 engines; extended wing-tips; new pressure fuel system; permanent scanner; additional tankage; all-up weight increased to 68,000 lb. BVIIs similar apart from their Hercules XVI engines and all-up weight of 65,000 lb.

HALIFAX CVIII

These transports carried passenger and freight and served as ambulances. Rearturrets replaced by farings; no additional guns; provision for 8,000 lb-capacity panniers; additional escape hatches and port-holes. Otherwise identical with BVI. Earlier Halifax transports: CIII (converted from BIII, scanners and guns being removed) and the similar CVI and CVII (converted from BVI and BVII).

HALIFAX AIX

Final Airborne Forces' aircraft. Similar to BVIIs; two 0.5-inch guns in rear turret; top turret removed abd structure continuous; large paratroop-door; additional escape hatch. Produced earlier; AIIIs (converted from BIIIs, with top-turret and scanner removed, extended wing-tips and increased tankage) and AVIIs (similar to AIIIs but converted from BVIIs).

PHOTO-LOFTING
Pioneered in Britain by Handley Page, the photo-lofting technique speeded Halifax production. Exact copies of the original design were circulated to daughter-firms and subcontractors. Complete inter-changeability of all components was ensured thereby.

Post-war Endeavour

Continued achievement has been the characteristic of the post-war era for Handley Page Ltd. In its works, a large-scale metamorphosis has resulted in the quantity production of new civil and military aircraft; research, design and development work have continued on new and advanced types of aeroplanes.

The Hermes, fully-pressurised and air-conditioned, is the latest civil transport which the Company is building. Britain's fastest long-range airliner, it is also the country's first big aircraft to have a tricycle undercarriage and is the most highly-powered in its class.

A large forty-passenger Hermes fleet is in full production for service with the British Overseas Airways Corporation on its main Empire routes.

These 37-ton airliners have a performance, and provide amenities and a degree of passenger comfort previously offered only in aircraft of much greater size. They have a maximum cruising speed of 290 mph, a payload of more than seven tons, a range in excess of 3,500 miles and, for high-density medium-range operations, carry seventy-four passengers.

Development of the Hermes range already is in an advanced stage of design and construction. This will result in new versions of the airliner whose keynote will be still higher performance and additional efficiency.

One, the Hermes V in the 40-74 passenger class, will be powered by Bristol Theseus propeller jet-turbines which provide nearly 10,000 equivalent take-off horsepower. It is designed for operation at the high flight levels associated with this form of power plant. Expected to be flying by the autumn of 1949, the Hermes V will cruise at six miles a minute and have a maximum range of 2,820 miles.

Hermes airliners are the civil developments of the new high-performance Hastings military transports which are in service with the RAF as Transport Command's standard long-range aircraft. They are the largest and fastest military transports to be built in Britain. Their full-scale production has been under way during the past two years.

NEW AND FAST
Britain's fastest long-range airliner, the Hermes is the latest civil transport which Handley Page is
building.

Hastings, operating on the Berlin airlift, have shown their ability to carry big loads
of heavy and cumbersome freight. This was an impressive contribution to Operation
Plainfare's success in the relief of the beleaguered German capital. Not only has each
transport carried in less than an hour eight tons of Ruhr coal to Berlin over the
210 miles from Kiel, but also the Hastings distinguished itself as a vehicle for the
RAF's biggest post-war passenger-lift to be scheduled from Berlin to the United
Kingdom.

With a top speed of 354 mph. and able to cruise at a maximum of 303 mph, the
Hastings has a service-ceiling of nearly 27,000 feet, an initial rate of climb at normal
climb power of 1,110 feet per minute and a range of 3,260 miles.

Its high-performance was demonstrated recently when the Hastings completed
a successful 35,000 miles global tour in which several speed records were broken. Its
operational characteristics were found to be excellent during 160 hours of intensive
flight in varied conditions of climate and altitudes. But, despite its excellent qualities,
developments of the Hastings directed towards still greater efficiency, are being
investigated by the Handley Page design team.

This versatile aircraft already has proved itself to be highly satisfactory in all of
its many operational roles which include freighter (with internally and externally
carried loads), paratrooper, ambulance, troop-transport, supplies-dropping aircraft
and tug capable of towing the largest glider.

Such equipment as bulldozers, 25-pounder guns and 3-ton lorries are air-
transportable up to a weight of eight tons. Both jeeps and guns can be dropped by
parachute. Facilitating their loading are a large freight door and a specially-constructed

DESIGNED FOR COMFORT
Hermes passenger cabins are pressurised, air-conditioned and extensively sound-proofed. Although the spacious fuselage could accommodate over seventy seats for short-range operations, in the version being supplied to BOAC only forty passengers will be carried, thereby giving extreme comfort on the long Empire routes.

ramp which is air-transportable. Fifty fully-equipped airborne troops are carried or, as an ambulance, the Hastings accommodates thirty-two stretcher and twenty-eight sitting cases, a medical officer, three nurses and a ton of medical supplies.

A subsidiary company, Handley Page (Reading) Ltd., at Woodley aerodrome in Berkshire, is operating an RAF Reserve Flying Training School and Communications Flight, is manufacturing the Miles Marathon four-engined feeder-line transport and is undertaking the repair and service of other types of Miles aircraft. Ample facilities exist there for the overhaul and maintenance of aircraft in all categories up to the big four-engined Hastings class.

The dual-purpose Marathon, in full production, has a very wide civil transport application and sales potential throughout the world.

In the medium-size range, the aircraft has an outstanding performance. It meets, and in some respects exceeds, the high standard of safety requirements now being introduced internationally. As an airliner, it has a 22-passenger capacity and, in its

A GRACEFUL APPROACH
Hermes is Britain's first big aircraft to have a tricycle undercarriage and is the most highly powered in its class.

freighter role, will carry a 2-ton low-density load. Military requirements are fulfilled by the Marathon as light-freighter and communications aircraft.

A pioneer of aeronautical research, Handley Page continues in the forefront of current developments with its forthcoming military and civil aircraft types of advanced conception and design.

They are in keeping with the modern trend which involves jet propulsion allied to swept-back, laminar-flow wings and tailless flight; they take into serious account the complexities of jet and rocket propulsion, of atomic power, of electronics and of new applications for materials and metals; they call for continuous research of materials, structures and equipment which will withstand the rigorous conditions pertaining to near-sub and supersonic regions of high-speed flight.

ON PARADE

Hastings, Britain's largest and fastest military transports, are being delivered to the RAF at an increasing rate from the Handley Page production lines.

LUXURY LAYOUT

A fleet of 25 Hermes IVs will be operated by BOAC on its Empire routes. In addition to the spacious flight-deck and passenger-cabins, there are generous toilet and cloakroom facilities and a large galley.

Orders have been received by Handley Page for new types of aircraft which represent the latest and most advanced in aeronautical endeavour. These, both in production and on the drawing-board as well as those in current operational service, have a unique heritage. They are the fruits of research which never ceases in the Handley Page organisation. From such efforts in the past have evolved renowned "firsts" in aviation history.

It was before the World War, in addition to its other experimental work at the time, that the Handley Page organisation began research into the problems concerned with tail-less flight. To this end, the Manx was designed and constructed. Research having started in 1937, the aircraft was ready for test-flying trials at the beginning of the war. Subsequently, because of the preoccupation of the Company with its massive bomber-building programme, tail-less research was slowed until 1945. Then the Manx, during extensive flying-tests, provided the Handley Page designers with comprehensive data in this sphere.

1952 AIRLINER TODAY
The Marathon, a product of Handley Page (Reading) Ltd., is a medium-range passenger/freighter whose performance exceeds I.C.A.O.'s proposed safety requirements for the future.

SUPPLIES DROPPING
Jeeps and supplies are slung beneath the Hastings in its supply-dropping role. Anti-tank guns, together with their crews, are dropped from the aircraft by parachute.

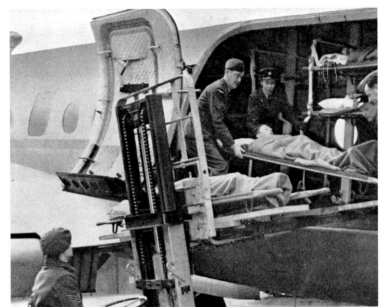

FLYING HOSPITAL
As an air-ambulance, the Hastings carries 32 stretcher and 28 sitting cases, a medical officer, nurses and a ton of medical supplies at high speed over long ranges.

MAID-OF-ALL-WORK
Cumbersome military equipment up to a total of 7½ tons is accommodated in the Hastings' fuselage which gives unrestricted freight-carrying space of 3,000 square feet. Standard long-range vehicle for RAF Transport Command, the Hastings' many roles include air-ambulance (1& 2), paratrooper (3 & 6), freighter (4) and troop transport (5).

FIRES FOR FRITZ
On the Berlin air-lift
and operating from
Schleswigland, each
Hastings flies the 210
miles to Germany's
capital in less than an
hour with eight tons
of Ruhr coal or other
heavy or bulky freight.

NAMESAKES
While on its visit
to the Antipodes,
a Hastings flew in
salute around a clock-
tower of the New
Zealand Hastings.

TAIL-LESS RESEARCH
Before the World War, Handley Page began research into tail-less flight. Its Manx was built but concentration upon bomber production slowed research until 1945 when intensive test-flying produced comprehensive data.

FUTURE TRENDS
Handley Page's forthcoming military and civil aircraft are of advanced conception and design.

Safety, a feature pioneered by the Company with its slotted-wing in 1919, is not being neglected in the ever-increasing demand for speed in the air. Means are being studied whereby the efficiency of high-lift devices may be increased still more in order to assist the take-off and landing qualities of very fast aircraft.

Handley Page's distinction, during the forty years of its existence, is of having combined pioneering with production and of having incorporated new ideas and sometimes fundamental new conceptions in its series-built aeroplanes. It is this pioneer-cum-production stamp which hallmarks every Handley Page aircraft, so often in the forefront of its contemporaries in flight.

In the military sphere, Handley Page led the way by producing the first big bomber. Since the days of the O/100, notable advances have been made by the Company in the development of the multi-engined bomber and military transport.

It is the honour of few aircraft manufacturers to introduce a new type of aeroplane into military service and to keep that type in continuous operation with the national air forces without intermission. That, though, is the Handley Page record.

From the Great War onwards, the Handley Page organisation, an integral part of national defence, has contributed largely to Britain's aerial striking power. Its bombers have been in constant service for more than three decades and at no period in its history has the RAF been without big Handley Page aeroplanes in service.

In the civil sphere, the Handley Page record is no less outstanding. Achievements have included the introduction and development in Britain of the multi-engined passenger aircraft, a type now universally accepted for all forms of commercial work; the study and production of a quiet and comfortable Pullman-type cabin for aerial passengers; the evolution of the high-payload airliner which can be operated at a profit.

Handley Page W/8 (and variants) and Hannibal/Heracles airliners were world-beaters in their days. Their success may be ascribed to the worthy experience which was gained when Handley Page Transport Ltd. pioneered and reigned supreme in the sphere of initial airline operations.

Complementary to this exceptional background of aircraft production and airline operation is the Handley Page research and development work which has given to the world not only the slotted-wing, and the flying safety bestowed by this invention, but much else besides.

Handley Page Ltd. can look back upon a period of successful aeroplane building and operation such as few other aviation concerns anywhere in the world can show. It has played an important part in the advancement of aeronautics. It can lay claim to an unusually high proportion of original work in the conception of new types of aircraft and in the production of new safety devices. It has made a distinguished contribution to victory in two world wars.

From humble beginnings, the advance of aviation has been paced by the pioneer work of the Handley Page organisation. The promise of atomic power, the application of rockets and jets as new propulsive media, the harnessing of electronics to the control of flight and the increasing suitability of materials and metals signify the wider scope of aviation in the future. Such developments are a spur to the Company's even greater efforts in the years to come.

Handley Page Ltd. never has held a stronger position than at present as it enters its forty-first year in the vanguard of aeronautical research, endeavour and achievement. It embarks upon the next four decades with sober satisfaction in its past accomplishments and with confidence in its products of to-day, in its plans for the future and in its ability to sustain British power in the air.

CRICKLEWOOD PRODUCTION
Hastings and Hermes aircraft, in full-scale production for the RAF and
BOAC, move along the busy assembly-lines at Handley Page's Cricklewood
works.

RADLETT ASSEMBLY
Major sections having been produced at Cricklewood by a technique akin
to mass-production, they are assembled finally at Radlett and the complete
aircraft test-flown

RADLETT 1949
All Handley Page's new aircraft are test-flown at the Company's Radlett aerodrome. There an experimental department, complete with modern wind-tunnel, is busy with research and builds prototype aircraft.

METAMORPHOSIS
Its main works at Cricklewood, its aerodrome and assembly-shops at Radlett and its subsidiary at Reading are tokens of the Handley Page organisation's present-day status in modern aeronautics and of its vast expansion since it began forty years ago, in the old ramshackle Barking works. This development of a pioneer company is symptomatic of the great progress which aviation has made in four triumphant decades of peace and war.

Handley Page's Four Decades of Achievement

1909 First limited liability aircraft-manufacturing company.

1909 First British works constructed solely for the production of aircraft.

1915 World's first successful big aeroplane — the O/100 or "Handley Page". Progenitor of modern heavy-bomber.

1916 Passenger-carrying record — 20 people airborne in an O/400, Britain's standard Great War bomber which attacked Germany and enemy naval forces.

1917 First flight from United Kingdom to any destination outside Europe — an O/400 flies to Egypt.

1917 First long-distance bombing raid — an O/400 flies 440 miles and attacks Constantinople.

1918 On its formation, the Independent Air Force's heavy bomber squadrons were composed of O/400s which attacked German Rhineland towns.

1918 First flight of V/1500, world's first 4-engined bomber. This "super Handley" was designed to bomb Berlin.

1918 World passenger-carrying record — 40 over London in V/1500.

1918 George VI and Duke of Windsor make their first cross-Channel flight in O/400 bomber.

1919 First aeroplane on cross-Channel passenger service-an O/400, converted to H.M. Air Liner "Silver Star", flies British delegates to Paris Peace Conference. Also operates first night passenger service to France.

1919 Handley Page Transport Ltd. starts one of Britain's first overseas airlines and carries majority of passengers to Continent.

1919 Invention of slotted-wing-revolutionary air-safety aid.

1920 Twin-engined W/8 easily wins highest award in Air Ministry's civil aviation competition and first prize for commercial aircraft at International Meeting in Brussels.

1922 Hanley, a torpedo carrier, is first aircraft specially designed for slots.

1924   Handley Page Transport Ltd. is nucleus around which British Government-sponsored Imperial Airways is founded.

1926   Imperial Airways' fleet composed of 65% Handley Page airliners which provided 70% of British airlines' total seating capacity.

1928   British Air Ministry orders Handley Page slots to be fitted to all RAF aircraft. Imperial Airways implement similar decision in regard to airliners.

1930   World's first 4-engined airliners — the Hannibal/Heracles class. Designed primarily for the passenger. In subsequent ten years, establish world record for safety and reliability in operation.

1931   Only two aircraft — both fitted with Handley Page slots — survive Guggenheim air-safety competition's stringent tests; one is Handley Page Gugnunc.

1936   World's introduction to split-construction and unit-assembly methods of aircraft production-originated and developed by Handley Page to achieve fast output of Harrow bomber.

1938   First use of split-construction in production of all-metal aeroplane — Hampden.

1939   Large production order for Halifax bomber placed before flight of prototype.

1940-1   "First off" Halifax flies; 5 weeks later, first Halifax squadron being formed; 4 months afterwards, Halifaxes make first operational sorties.

1944   Halifax only aircraft able to tow World War's largest, tank-carrying gliders.

1946   Last Halifax built. In all, 6,176 produced; represent more than 40% of Britain's total wartime heavy-bomber power. Twenty-six major variants operated in 6 different combat roles.

1946   Production commences of Hastings, Britain's largest and fastest military transport, as standard long-range vehicle for RAF Transport Command.

1948   First flight of Hermes IV, Britain's fastest airliner and first 4-engined aircraft with a tricycle undercarriage.

1948-9   Hastings and Halifaxes carry large proportion of British load on Berlin air-lift.